EDGE OF AWE

EDGE OF AWE

Experiences of the Malheur-Steens Country

Edited by **Alan L. Contreras**

Foreword by **William Kittredge**

Illustrations by **Ursula K. Le Guin**

Oregon State University Press   Corvallis

Library of Congress Cataloging-in-Publication Data

Names: Contreras, Alan, 1956– editor. | Kittredge, William, writer of
   foreword. | Le Guin, Ursula K., 1929–2018, illustrator.
Title: Edge of awe : experiences of the Malheur-Steens country / edited by
   Alan L. Contreras ; foreword by William Kittredge ; illustrations by
   Ursula K. Le Guin.
Description: Corvallis : Oregon State University Press, 2019.
Identifiers: LCCN 2018055142 | ISBN 9780870719615 (original trade pbk. : alk.
   paper)
Subjects: LCSH: Natural history—Oregon. | Malheur National Wildlife
   Refuge (Or.)
Classification: LCC QH105.O7 E33 2019 | DDC 508.795—dc23
LC record available at https://lccn.loc.gov/2018055142

♾ This paper meets the requirements of ANSI/NISO Z39.48-1992
(Permanence of Paper).

Oregon State University
OSU Press

Oregon State University Press
121 The Valley Library
Corvallis OR 97331-4501
541-737-3166 • fax 541-737-3170
www.osupress.oregonstate.edu

Dedicated to the Wadatika (Burns Paiute) tribe
and all members of the Harney County community, including
the professional staff of the Malheur National Wildlife Refuge,
the Bureau of Land Management, and other public employees, volunteers,
and visitors who work together to manage the lands, waters,
and unique natural world of the Malheur–Steens region in trust
for all people who would learn what the region has to teach.

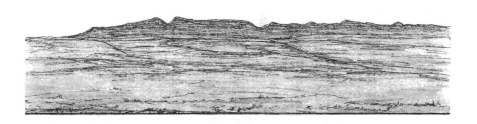

This vast open can't quite be named. It stays always one step ahead of the namers, luring us who would try deeper and deeper into its embrace.

— Ellen Waterston

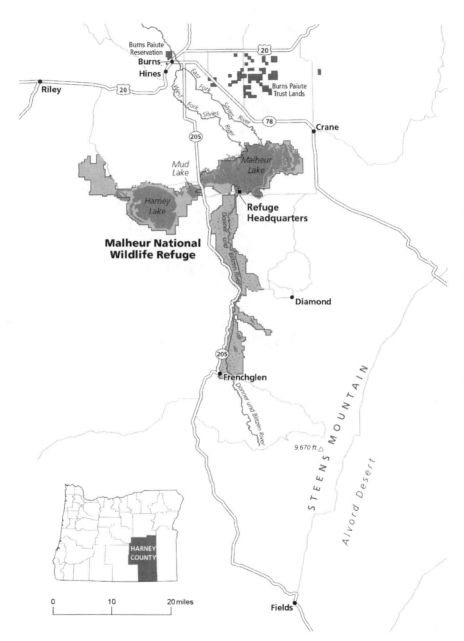

Cartography by InfoGraphics Lab, Department of Geography, University of Oregon.

CONTENTS

PART 3: DESERT PILGRIMAGE

WILLIAM KITTREDGE

Foreword: The Steens and Malheur

In the summer of 1943 I was eleven. My cattle ranching family had sent me out with the MC buckaroos. They were branding calves on the Great Basin deserts of southeastern Oregon and northern Nevada, traveling the sagebrush, lava-rock plains with a four-horse chuck wagon on two-track roads that led them from one line camp (water hole) to the next.

We were set up in the early morning darkness at South Corral, a circular rock-wall enclosure built before World War II by mustang runners. Our horsemen were up and readying for another long-distance day when I was startled by a burst of incandescence that was falling through a V-shaped slot at the otherwise utterly black summit of Steens Mountain (the largest fault-block in North America).

Irreligious as I was, the sun, its sudden light, to a boy a long way from his mother and home, seemed to be threatening, frightening, after me and dangerous. I had been sent out to toughen up with those hard-handed men and their soon-to-be-lost codes and the myths of cattle ranching. My family ranch, the MC, after we had delivered six thousand mother cows, was sold in 1967. Our lives, in our electronic worlds, everywhere, are not like they were in 1943. Not any more.

In 1872, at the age of twenty-three, Peter French went to work for Doctor Hugh Glenn, a California cattle baron whose pastures ran for miles along the Sacramento River. Leading six vaqueros and a Chinese cook, Charlie On Long, young Peter French was put in charge of driving twelve hundred head of Doctor Glenn's livestock north into the deserts of southeastern Oregon, where grazing lands were rumored to be free for the taking. And, indeed, they were.

Driving that herd across what eventually became MC rangelands, passing South Corral, they found abundant water and meadows just where the slope of Steens Mountain begins rising, at Roaring Springs. On north, over a small rise, Peter French sat looking out at a free-for-the-taking reach of swampland and pasture that was watered by the Donner und Blitzen River after it emerged from a glacial cirque that reached into the heart of Steens Mountain. There, he found the P Ranch—his soon-to-be-empire, waiting and ready.

The legendary P Ranch lasted and expanded until one day after Christmas in 1897. Working cattle in his northern fields, at the Sod House, French was shot dead by homesteader Ed Oliver, and the P Ranch began ending. I have to conjecture about those slate-eyed citizens like Peter French and my grandfather. Did they actually believe they could mold their world around conquest patterns they'd observed while herding?

After graduation from Oregon State and marriage and children and wasted years in the Strategic Air Command, by the 1960s I was back on the MC—the most extensive (nineteen thousand irrigated acres) of the ranches assembled by my grandfather—directing the haying in alfalfa fields and the barley farming.

Steens Mountain, off to the east, lay beyond the million acres of desert grazing lands my family leased from the national government. That world, out in the far side of the eleven long-abandoned homesteader post offices that lasted a few years in Catlow Valley, so far as I knew, existed in mystery.

So, a bookish man of the sort that seeks out information, on an October day after the barley harvest was finished and the John Deere 36 combines had been put away for another year, I went to Steens, wanting to see it from close up, exploring south of Burns, a Harney County ranching and lumber mill town of the sort I'd grown up understanding.

After the alkaline distances of Malheur Lake, I turned onto a gravel roadway over the eroding bluffs that run along on the border of the northern division of the old P Ranch. My grandfather had leased those acres

just as the Great Depression was getting underway. Oscar Kittredge, my
father, told of the winter of 1929. He'd lived alone out there in the fall-
ing-down Sod House, looking after steers and heifers that belonged to
his father.

But, to my grandfather's cattle rancher dismay, the Sod House division
of the P Ranch was sold (for $67,000 as I recall) to the government and
folded into the Malheur Wildlife Refuge, which had been established by
Teddy Roosevelt in 1908 (since then it's grown to 187,000 acres). Seeking
to replace the grazing for his far-too-many cows, my grandfather bought
the MC Ranch in Warner Valley.

While I could sort of remember that boyhood morning out at South
Corral, I knew little about Steens Mountain and the P Ranch and the
Malheur Wildlife Refuge. There was plenty to witness and learn from.

Driving through the watered and sometimes swampy interior of the
refuge, I spooked herds of mule deer and passed silent, long-legged herons as they stalked, and trumpeter swans and red-tailed hawks and one
falcon before the end of my afternoon, when I wandered through French's
headquarters, where he built his long barn and woven-willow corrals and
put up his white-painted, two-story house while his vaqueros were driving yearly herds of steers and heifers to the railroad in Winnemucca. This
was where he lived while assembling his seventy-two thousand acres (he'd
bought forty-two thousand acres in the Diamond Valley, hayfields, for a
dollar an acre).

That night I put up in the French Glenn Hotel (rib steak and bour-
bon for dinner). In the morning I was up early and pleased by the odor of
sagebrush and meadow hay while roosters crowed and a flight of darting
green-winged teal dropped toward a roadside slough.

Since the summit of the Steens was glittering with early snow, and
the fifty-two mile loop road around the top was barricaded and closed, I
turned north toward Barton Lake and the locally famous round barn that
French had caused to be built (there had been another, torn down long
before). Arrows of sunlight shone inside over luminous juniper rafters
that converged into an intricate, churchlike crown. Those round barns had
sheltered French's horse-breaking vaqueros through winters. Returning, I
was in Warner by nightfall. French and his P Ranch became one of my
obsessions.

In 1980, gone from Warner Valley (my family had mainly sold our ranches in 1967), hoping to expand my relationship (I was teaching in Montana) to my old territory, I invited my daughter Karen and her husband, Daryl, and their infant, Zach, and my brother Pat and sister Roberta and true companion, Annick Smith, with her twin sons Alex and Andrew (thirteen and into arcane baseball statistics, like the Willie Mays batting average the day he retired) to a family gathering at a BLM campground beside Fish Lake, almost at the summit.

After unloading, it was nearing twilight when we rushed up to the top. An abrupt edge just above the roadway (I drove Annick's SUV on up there, nearly over, way too excited), fell from where we stood, a four-thousand-foot rockfall to Alvord Lake. Miles beyond lay the White Horse Ranch (the initial ranch in that country, organized by another California man, John Devine, three years before French and still prospering).

Looking west from that elevation we could see patterns in the old MC rangelands (including South Corral), and all the way to Hart Mountain, which loomed at the north end of Warner. On a clear day, we were told, it's possible to identify mountaintops in five different states (one of them, Bidwell Mountain in California, was just south of Warner, and another, of course, was where we stood on the Steens).

The next morning, on our way to the summit we stopped at a lush grassland with groves of white-barked aspen, Whorehouse Meadow (that name was ridiculously changed, by the BLM, to Naughty Girl Meadow. Following widespread local laughter, mapmakers renamed it Whorehouse Meadow). The history there went back to around 1900 when maybe ten thousand sheep were summering in those highlands. Towns like Burns emptied out because so many men had gone to the mountain, where they were herding. Enterprising women loaded wagons and took themselves to their customers, setting up camps in those meadows. The herders had awkwardly carved signs and signals—wine glasses and vaginas and narratives like Eddy + Rebecca—into the aspen trees. After dissuading my son-in-law, Daryl, from hiking the entire rough-country length of Kiger Gorge to hayfields in the vicinity of the Diamond store, we contented ourselves with hiking the edges of glacial cirques and sipping pretty good wines, toasting paradise.

As Bill Clinton's tenure was ending in 1999, two kinds of citizens, each group thinking that control of the Malheur Wildlife Refuge and the highlands of Steens Mountain was vitally significant in their lives, were facing down over the fact that they seriously disagreed about who should own and/or manage those territories.

Ranchers on Steens Mountain, families that had been located for generations, owned well over two hundred thousand acres and ran about eighteen thousand head of cattle. They were mightily concerned about protecting their property rights in general and for sure their inherited ways of life. But environmentalists, often from urban centers, had found and learned to cherish spectacular local landscapes and honor the necessity of maintaining nesting grounds for the hundreds of thousands of water birds that annually came in from the Pacific Flyway.

Politicians worked at finding a compromise. After input from all sides, they actually did. Their agreement passed through Congress and in October 2000 was signed into law by Bill Clinton. While that did not end the conflicts, it established a framework for cooperation that held up until January 2016, when armed, out-of-state protesters seized the refuge headquarters and demanded that the federal government give up control of public land. After their leaders were arrested and one of them was killed, they surrendered.

This outburst of rebellious lawlessness reminded me of the "Sagebrush Rebellion" that briefly raged across the West in the early 1980s. I was invited to contribute a response. My anti-rebellion argument centered on the notion that turning federal lands in the West over to private individuals would lock local citizens into bondage, limiting freedoms. Would cattlemen end up owning Steens Mountain? Not likely. The very wealthy, the billionaires, would own whatever they wanted to own, particularly the spectacular properties like the Steens and the Malheur.

"The one process that will take millions of years to correct," E. O. Wilson wrote, "is the loss of genetic and species diversity by the destruction of natural habitats. It is the folly our descendants are least likely to forgive us." That insight takes me to Ursula K. Le Guin, illustrator of this book, who responded while looking out from a location on McCoy Creek, hoping her patient wisdom would reassure and invigorate all of us, every-where on this sacred earth.

PETER PEARSALL

Preface

Malheur is a special place, for so many reasons and for so many people. It seems to have an indelible effect on its visitors, as evidenced by the variety of essays, memoirs, and poems—a body of remembrance spanning several decades—that graces this volume. First-time visitors to the area tend to come away awed, even reverent, and eager to return. I freely admit that I am a Malheur neophyte. I first visited the refuge in 2015, was absolutely gobsmacked by what I saw, and returned several times in 2017, ultimately assuming the role of executive director with Friends of Malheur National Wildlife Refuge.

I came to the high desert on a whim. I craved a change: change of scenery, of pace, of overall milieu. Coming from the verdant and increasingly populous Pacific Northwest, I was utterly naive about what awaited me east of the mountains. My head was filled with sandy notions, preconceived and ill informed. Sure, people had told me what to expect, but this in no way prepared me for the stark reality of *living* it. I was told to expect heat, wide-open spaces, and recluse-worthy solitude. I was told to drink lots of water and wear sunscreen. I was told that the desert was no place to get lost or stranded or stuck, because the desert was a merciless place, unforgiving in the extreme.

I worked for two field seasons in Nevada's Black Rock Desert-High Rock Canyon-Emigrant Trails National Conservation Area in 2013 and 2014, first with the Bureau of Land Management and then with Friends of Black Rock-High Rock, a conservation-based nonprofit in the area. In emigrant journal entries about the area, I learned of the myriad hardships faced by westering travelers and settlers in the late nineteenth century. Archaeological texts informed my understanding of the region's indigenous groups, their traditions dating back thousands of years and perpetuated by present-day tribal members. Their ancestors led an austere and itinerant existence, living by what scant resources the desert deigned to offer up through the seasons.

I marveled at descriptions of the xeric biota, resourceful to a fault. "The desert, the dry and sun-lashed desert, is a good school in which to observe the cleverness and the infinite variety of techniques of survival under pitiless opposition," wrote John Steinbeck in *Travels with Charley*. "Life could not change the sun or water the desert, so it changed itself. . . . The desert has mothered magical things."

But there's a lot to the high desert I wasn't apprised of beforehand. No one told me about the spectacular moonrises over the desert, for instance, or the spiraling ecliptic of planets and stars and galaxies that lit up the night sky whenever I chanced to look up. No one told me about the summer storms that boil up darkly from the west, dumping in an hour's time more than an inch of rain across the desert and then dissipating, the wind scouring the sky clear of cloud as if nothing happened, the sagebrush afterward so fragrant and dewed. No one said the wild horses might sometimes race alongside my bicycle on the highway, gamely keeping pace for a couple dozen yards before turning off, shaking their manes and tails and watching me pedal on. Not once did anyone venture the possibility that I might come to enjoy the desert; that I might find facets within to inspire an abiding love and respect for it. Those I discovered on my own.

I've since made my home in the high desert of Harney County, working to assist Malheur Refuge staff in protecting and enhancing the area's ample natural resources for the benefit of wildlife and wildlife admirers alike. I thought that my experience in the Black Rock Desert region would somehow prepare me for what Malheur had to offer, but I was wrong. I had indulged in the very same stereotyping that I railed against while encountering first-time visitors in the Black Rock region—that is, I had over-generalized the desert, obscuring its complexity with landscape-scale assumptions.

I'm beginning to find that Malheur is as distinct a place as the Black Rock Desert was to me when I first experienced it, back in 2013 as a coastal transplant. Perhaps more so, because Malheur enjoys the distinction of being a high-desert oasis for wildlife, an ecological jewel along the Pacific Flyway when such refuges for migratory birds are few and far between. It is a place that, through its subtle charms and hard-won acquaintance, speaks volumes to people and stays with them wherever they go. I suspect that the longer I spend delving into the intricacies of this place, the deeper my conviction will grow.

Peter Pearsall served as executive director of the Friends of Malheur National Wildlife Refuge from 2017 to 2018.

ALAN L. CONTRERAS

Introduction

"Malheur" is the one-word answer that many people in the Northwest give when asked about their favorite location to watch birds and other wildlife. But what is Malheur, exactly? At the core of what we think of as the "Malheur experience" is the formal entity known as Malheur National Wildlife Refuge. The refuge is a T-shaped array of sage steppe, marshland, and river valley with shallow Malheur Lake as its largest and most iconic feature.

Then there is the mountain. The vast tilted massif of Steens Mountain, widely and colloquially known as "The Steens" even though it is essentially one geologic object, hangs on the refuge's southeastern horizon like a grandparent who keeps watch on the rambunctious Donner und Blitzen River and all that it waters. From a distance, the mountain's enormity is obscured, its undulating waves of aspen invisible, its glacial canyons unsuspected, its hawks, hummingbirds, deer, and hillsides of flowers only imagined.

There is no other place in the Northwest, and few anywhere, like the Malheur-Steens complex. The ultimate pilgrimage for Oregon birders and one that is immensely satisfying for anyone interested in the natural world, Malheur National Wildlife Refuge lies at four thousand feet in the high desert at the northern end of the Great Basin. The Great Basin is sometimes thought of as an empty place, even a sterile place. The desert is neither empty nor sterile; indeed, it is full of life adapted to its requirements. Malheur, though, provides that astonishing change agent: *water.* In some years there isn't much; in other years there is too much.

And then there is the east side of Steens Mountain. The Alvord Desert and its unique dry habitats are a source of great enjoyment for thousands of tourists as well as home for ranch families on the greener slopes. The isolated community of Fields anchors the southern edge of the Malheur experience and offers a gateway to the desert ranges extending south to Nevada. This latter area, south of the refuge proper, is seeing more tourist activity despite its remoteness.

One reason that the refuge is special to so many people is that it is rather isolated, three hundred miles from Oregon's population centers, hemmed in on three sides by cliffs and hills, with the vast shield of Steens Mountain filling the sky to the southeast, providing part of the valley's water from snowmelt. Away from the northern part of the refuge, many cell phones reach nothing, and a person who chooses to be alone in the desert or valley can do so most of the year.

Each small place in this huge land seems to be an essential part of the whole for many visitors. For forty-nine years I have stood on the same rocks, by mostly the same trees, with the same views and essentially the same trails. The stroll into Benson Pond (formerly a drive). The experience of entering the wooded compound at refuge headquarters on an early June dawn, when the urgency of life can be seen, heard, and felt in the air. The campground and river at Page Springs. The pointillist views of the Fish Creek basin in early October. The unexpected awe of looking down Kiger Gorge or up Little Blitzen. The extraordinary silence of mid-autumn in the groves or on the playa. The waving curtain of sound in the marshes in late spring. The clarity of January air looking from the northern valley all the way to the mountain.

Then there are the people and what they bring to the space. The Frenchglen store and neighborhood. The iconic face of Roaring Springs Ranch gazing across the Catlow valley. The isolated welcomes of Fields Station and the Diamond Hotel. The unique decrepit glory of the Malheur Field Station, base point of thousands of visits and visitors. The staff and volunteers at Malheur National Wildlife Refuge headquarters. Malheur is one of those places that is far greater than the sum of its parts.

Dave Marshall, senior editor of *Birds of Oregon* (OSU Press, 2003), first went to Malheur in 1936. It was a two-and-a-half-day marathon just to *get* there from Portland over endless gravel and dirt roads, much as Dallas Lore Sharp described in *Where Rolls the Oregon*:

> The trail takes account of every possible bunch of sagebrush and greasewood to be met with on the way. It never goes over a bunch if it can go around a bunch; and as there is nothing but bunches all the way, the road is very devious. It turns, here and there, every four or five feet (perhaps the sagebrush clumps average five feet apart), and it has a habit, too whenever it sees the homesteader's wire fences, of dashing for them, down one side of the claim, then short about the corner and down the other side of the claim, steering clear of all the clumps of sage, but ripping along horribly near to the sizzling barbs of the wire and the untrimmed stubs on the juniper posts; then darting off into the brush, this way, that way, every way, which in the end proves to be the way to Burns, but no one at the beginning of the trip could believe it— no one from the East, I mean. . . .
>
> It was 7:10 in the morning when we started from Bend, it was after eight in the evening when we swung into Burns.

Dave's trip at age eleven was a precursor or premonition: Dave became refuge biologist and worked at Malheur from 1955–1960. I first visited at fourteen in 1970 and Matt Hunter, the third coeditor of *Birds of Oregon*, at sixteen in 1980. Such is the magnetism of this pilgrimage.

Why? What is so special about Malheur that brings us back to the mosquitoes, the dust, the hard water, flat tires, and thunderstorms? Most of all, there are the birds. It is likely that more species of birds can be seen and heard from the front lawn of Malheur headquarters than from any other single location where an observer can stand in Oregon, perhaps in the whole northwestern quarter of North America. Every migrant passerine species crossing the Great Basin, with a few exceptions that use only specialized habitat, stops in the horseshoe of trees that shelters the headquarters complex.

Even some of the supposedly specialized species stop in—for example, the canyon wren that spent a day exploring the roof of the bunkhouse and the flammulated owl that briefly and incongruously occupied a ground squirrel hole in the sage by the parking lot. Every water bird, hawk, owl, and hummingbird that passes through eastern Oregon is probably visible at some time from the headquarters lawn, either in the large pond right below the lawn or in the lake itself, visible by scope in the distance.

Only at a few places can the Northwest produce a movement of migrants reminiscent of the "waves" so prevalent in the eastern United States. In addition to the immense migratory flow of normal northwestern species through headquarters, vagrants from elsewhere in North America are found here more often than in any other Northwest location. Such unlikely visitors as the worm-eating warbler, yellow-throated vireo, and streak-backed oriole have appeared in these trees.

Why? The headquarters complex is an oasis in two kinds of desert, a rare situation that acts as a magnet for any bird passing through the region. It is an oasis of trees in a region dominated largely by sagebrush desert with a few alfalfa fields. It is also an oasis of land bordered on the north by what is, in some years, the largest lake in Oregon. Any bird crossing that lake from the north will head for the one large grove of trees on its shore. Any bird starting to cross that lake from the south in adverse weather conditions may well change its mind and double back to the shelter of the grove.

The Malheur Field Station is a collection of old Civilian Conservation Corps buildings and Eisenhower-gothic house trailers apparently dropped from the sky onto bare sage desert a few miles from refuge headquarters. A May morning starts very early at the field station. Long before daylight—indeed, before there is any apparent light at all—swallows start zipping around the buildings, calling loudly. They usually drown out the sage thrashers, which sometimes start singing earlier (if they bothered to stop at all during the night) but which are usually farther away. By the time most observers have staggered to breakfast and commented on how cold a May morning can be at four thousand feet, every other creature has stirred.

These mornings are even more spectacular in the marshes and at headquarters, where the sheer variety of sounds can be overwhelming as the singing imperative takes over and spring is declared for all comers to hear. Walking into the headquarters complex at dawn in late spring is one of the great anticipatory moments in an Oregon birder's life: What has arrived overnight? What strange and exciting song might herald a rare vagrant? And best of all, if you get there early enough when it is still chilly, most of the mosquitoes have not yet emerged from the grass.

For some of us, Malheur in the fall has equal charms as a birding destination and a place for contemplation. For in the fall, if you go to the field station or any other reasonably isolated place, you will hear that rarest of sounds in our modern world: silence. An evening at the field station in late September, when most of the tourists have gone and only a few birders are around, can be a time of extraordinary beauty and quiet, when literally no sounds can be heard for many long minutes, even half an hour or more. There is just the sky, the sage, the backdrop of Steens Mountain, and the occasional rabbit passing by.

STEENS MOUNTAIN

"Mother of waters and father of storms." That is how my poem entitled "Steens Mountain" begins. It is those things, but, from a distance, the mountain as seen from the west does not seem that impressive. Sure, there is snow on it most of the year, but then the valley floor below it lies at four thousand feet, so snow does not seem like that big a deal. And it has an interesting craggy skyline. So what's the excitement?

For someone who never leaves the Blitzen Valley during a visit to Malheur, Steens Mountain can appear to be simply a backdrop, more interesting than sky but basically just painted onto the cloud flow. You can read in refuge literature that the mountain provides a lot of the water that allows the refuge to live, yet this is simply another fact among many facts. It is the sheer scale of the mountain, combined with its origin, that allow it to stay in the background for those who do not consider it worth a closer look.

First of all, it does not look like any of Oregon's other high mountains. The higher Cascade peaks are classic volcanic cones that cumulate in a defined point and rise majestically (or at least distinctively in the case of extrusive Mount Washington and indicative Three Fingered Jack) over the surrounding terrain. The Wallowas are not volcanic but they, too, have in significant measure the properties of loftiness and grandeur that we expect of mountains. Steens Mountain does not look like this—at first.

Fault blocks such as Steens arise as a result of tectonic pressures, and there is some variation in how they look. Steens Mountain is a classic fault block, and a large one. Its basic formation extends more than fifty miles in a rough north-south direction. From the west—the direction from which most people see it—the mountain's size is not readily apparent, due to the gradualness of its rise, the intervening cliffs that hide it from the traveler's view, and the way its northern end curves to the east. Yet its summit ridge lies at an elevation over nine thousand feet and its highest point just under ten thousand feet.

It is from the east that the sheer mass of the mountain is most apparent. Seen from the Alvord Desert from Highway 95 or Whitehorse Ranch Road, it is by far the most dominant feature of the landscape, rising five thousand feet almost sheer from the floor of the Alvord and extending unbroken to the north and south, a primal wall that makes the Blitzen Valley a riparian garden and much of southeastern Oregon a drier desert where kit fox, leopard lizard, cacti, black-throated sparrows, and other species more common in the southern Great Basin can be found. There are even indigenous fish here: trout and the Borax Lake chub.

Yet even this view does not give you the true mountain, the uniqueness of its towering presence over all of southeastern Oregon. To know the mountain you must go upon it. The road up Steens Mountain is usually open from late June through October, depending on snow levels. Its lower section does not immediately impress the observer: instead of a flat expanse of sagebrush, there is a sloping expanse of sagebrush. Sometimes sage grouse can be seen here. Soon a dense juniper forest clothes the view. In fall, these stands are an important food source for migrant Townsend's solitaires and robins, which eat the berries.

The slope is easy but the climb is steady, and after a couple of miles in the juniper stands, the expanse of the upper mountain is suddenly closer, its massive shoulders partly hidden behind bluffs as the road winds through several small basins. The first stands of aspen appear above the juniper zone, strung along where there is a little more water: at the base of low rounded hills, in creek bottoms, around grassy sinks. After a while the sheer *volume* of aspen on the mountain becomes apparent: great sheets ripple on the hillsides, endless fingers probe every distant rivulet and cranny. And still the massif rises and spreads to the horizon north and south.

Above the lake basins as the trees thin and give way to grass and sage-brush, the number of breeding species—avian, mammalian, and every-thing else—is quite low owing to the limited habitat. Yet it is just here, as the "habitat" seems to be disappearing and the dominance of sheer stone becomes overwhelming, that Steens Mountain offers its greatest wonders to an observer. In late summer and early fall, these grassy, stony ridges offer a look at a phenomenon not easily observed in the western states' heavily forested mountains: the southward migration of hummingbirds and of hawks.

Sitting on the rocks at the head of Kiger Gorge to watch these birds is something I do not do very often. There is just you and the gorge:

Kiger Gorge

September is October
on the brink of the rim
but not yet in the canyon
where butter-tipped aspen
could be stalks of ripe mullein
but for ravens above them.

Pink-lined capes of tired snow
thrown back upon stone shoulders,
ravines revealed, blossom-edged
black finches on fissures
testing stone gateways,
seeking and swarming.

The edge of awe awaits
watchers on the cliff
there is no rail
just the air
below us
forever.

Kiger Gorge itself is perhaps the greatest visual wonder on the mountain. Completely invisible from the west, it is a glacially scooped valley with a creek and aspen along the bottom. From the overlook at its headwall, everything fifteen hundred feet below has a toylike, miniaturized quality that extends into the far distance before curving slightly to the west. If there are no tourists around, you can hear a low purr from the gorge, the distant sound of the creek and the wind in the aspen, with the occasional croak of a raven drifting across the canyon.

THE DESERT VISIONS OF URSULA K. LE GUIN

The recent passing of Ursula K. Le Guin provides an occasion to look through a unique window into both the Malheur region and the creative process. Le Guin first started visiting Harney County in the 1960s and was a regular visitor for decades, staying at the Malheur Field Station and later for many years at a private ranch near Diamond. I knew her for about twenty years mainly through our common interest in the Great Basin. We first met at the Wild Arts Festival in Portland in the 1990s. On one occasion we discussed the unique views from all kinds of observation points around the Blitzen Valley. Many of these images were set

forth in the book *Out Here*, which she did with Roger Dorband in 2010. Le Guin provided some short essays, poems, and line art while Dorband showcased his large color photos of the region. In her introduction to this book she wrote: "I first went to this high desert country over forty years ago. I remember a late evening walk up the wild slope behind the Frenchglen Hotel: the fragrance of sagebrush, the strange, dry, dangerous ground, the vast, clear sky above profiled buttes and the long, far ridge of the mountain."

What I had not realized until I read *Out Here* was that many of the scenes of the physical setting in the second of the Earthsea books, *The Tombs of Atuan*, were based on what she had seen while clambering around on the rough hillsides above Frenchglen. Our Malheur was thus immortalized in the form of scenes from a fictional desert on another planet.

There are many Malheur-specific poems in her collections. One of these, "Up in a Cottonwood" (see page 102), has always been a favorite because it does what she did so well: look at a scene from an unexpected point of view. In this case the view was through the eyes of one of the great horned owls at headquarters. She imagined them sneering at the bird-watchers below and wishing that they were slightly smaller so they could be eaten. Its last line is the perfect "An owl is mostly air." This poem is reprinted in this anthology. She also wrote poems about the field station and specific features found on the refuge.

Ursula was known as a writer, but she also immortalized Malheur and Steens Mountain (and the McCoy Creek Ranch where she stayed) in a series of very good drawings that appear in *Out Here*, some of which are reproduced in this anthology. Her introduction to *Out Here* ends with the revelation of what the Milky Way looks like at night from the high desert: ". . . it was eternity made visible. I was seeing, for once, with my mortal eyes, what is always here."

Few had her vision. She helped us all see what is and what could be. She still does.

ABOUT *EDGE OF AWE*

This collection offers the reader a sense of the sheer impact of Malheur and the extraordinary variety of intense personal experiences that people

have had in this harsh and splendid landscape. Oregon has some spectacular places—Crater Lake, the Wallowa Mountains, the Columbia Gorge,
Hells Canyon, the mouth of the Columbia River, and Cape Blanco come
to mind—but it is fair to say that few places in Oregon have generated
the sheer volume of commentary and varied emotional responses as has
the Malheur-Steens region.

Edge of Awe came to be as a result of conversations beginning in 2016
between the collection editor and the staff of OSU Press, members of the
Oregon birding community, and the staff of Malheur National Wildlife Refuge. Though primarily focused on the Malheur-Steens region as a
natural space, in sharing their reactions to this unique region, the writers
and artists bring the human experience. As is true of all things in Harney
County, thousands of people have, each in their own way, made the region
what it is as a human space.

The book is primarily about the experiences of *visitors* to the Malheur-
Steens region. It does not include the experiences of the Paiute people
who lived here for thousands of years. They were granted a 1.5 million
acre reservation in 1879, but Congress did not ratify President Grant's
proposal and after a series of battles, survivors from various tribes were
sent in a forced march to what amounted to a long-term holding pen near
Yakama, Washington. *Edge of Awe* also barely touches the experiences of
the people who now *live* in this region of Oregon. Though much remains
to be told, some of that story is told elsewhere. Three books that many
people have enjoyed are Nancy Langston's *Where Land and Water Meet*,
C.D. Littlefield's *Birds of Malheur National Wildlife Refuge* (which also
discusses the general biology of the region), and the enormous, beauti-
fully illustrated *Steens Mountain in Oregon's High Desert Country* by E. R.
Jackman and John Scharff. An interesting story of growing up in the
region is *Child of Steens Mountain* by Eileen O'Keefe McVicker. Finally,
Peter Walker's *Sagebrush Collaboration* (Oregon State University Press,
2018) discusses in some detail both the Bundy takeover and some of the
tribal responses.

I have not changed bird names or place names in previously published
essays to conform with current usage. In a couple of cases when a modern
reader might be confused, an explanatory note is added. Likewise, when a

writer's reference was unduly obscure, an additional word or two has been added in brackets. Throughout, common bird names are not capitalized.

I group the essays in three sections that are roughly chronological and also broadly represent three periods in human experience of the region: the time before the refuge, the refuge-building period, and the modern period of tourism. In a couple of cases in which an essay refers to an earlier time, I located the essays in a way that made the most sense to me. Poems appear between the essays with some sense of connection to adjacent essays but without regard to when they were written. I've prefaced many of the pieces with brief introductory notes.

I thank Nathan Williams and Hendrik Herlyn for retyping older works and transcribing videos for use in this collection. In addition, the staff of OSU Press has been very patient as this egg took a while to hatch. The two external reviewers who commented on the first draft were exceptionally perceptive about many issues, in particular how the various segments fit together. Many of us have our own unique and memorable experiences of this special region of the west. I hope that for those who have had many experiences at Malheur—and for those contemplating their first visit—this collection will provide inspiration and a sense of the timelessness of the natural world compared to the mayflies of human endeavor.

All royalties earned by this book will be paid to the Friends of Malheur National Wildlife Refuge to support projects such as trails, informative kiosks and the like on the refuge.

PART 1

State of Nature

The Harney Basin has been inhabited by people for thousands of years. Here Peter Walker begins the story of human experiences of Malheur with the earliest known Paiute inhabitants, then shares what happened as Anglo settlers started coming into the basin. Later in this collection you can read Greg Bryant's story of archaeological expeditions in the 1970s.

PETER WALKER

The Paiute Experience

My people fought hard for this land, I would never leave it, for the earth was my mother and the wind is my brother. —Paiute elder[1]

According to some tribal members, the Wadatika band of the northern Paiute have been in what is today Harney County, Oregon, since time immemorial.[2] According to academic archaeologists, ancestors of these people, commonly known today as the Burns Paiute, have likely been in the region for at least 14,500 years[3]—making southeast Oregon the oldest directly dated site of human occupation in the Western Hemisphere (Jenkins et al. 2012; Jenkins et al. 2013). Whether recorded by Paiute oral history or by traces of human DNA measured by radiocarbon dating, Native American people have been in southeastern Oregon a very long time.

Before the arrival of Euro-American settlers in large numbers in the second half of the nineteenth century, Paiute people traveled widely throughout the region in small family groups, camping near creeks, springs, and marshes (Aikens and Couture 1991). In the warmer months they moved frequently, following the seasonal abundance of fish, birds, rabbits, reptiles, rodents, deer, elk, and mountain sheep, and gathering a wide variety of plants, seeds, berries, roots, and bulbs (Louie 1989). Roots and fish were dried and placed in storage for the harsh winter months.[4] Family groups joined during periods of peak abundance for communal hunts, harvest of seeds, roots, and berries, and for celebrations (Langston 2003, 29). The region's rich lakes, rivers, streams, marshes, hillsides, meadows, and desert were all part of native people's shared home, livelihoods, and culture; permanent individual land ownership was unheard of (Burns Paiute Tribe 1995).

The diet and nomadic lifestyle of the Paiute were attuned to the natural productivity and variability of the desert environment and water sources—a fact that was, tragically, used by Euro-Americans to help justify the near-eradication of Paiute people. Whereas whites saw the Harney Basin as a desolate landscape in need of modification, control (especially water), and settlement, the Paiutes adapted to the region's ever-shifting abundance through mobility. To the Paiute, permanent settlements, material accumulation, and cultivation were impediments. Easily moveable shelters were built with lightweight willow, aspen, tules, and wild rye. To Euro-Americans, however, this mobility (and, ironically, the sophisticated local knowledge that made it possible) was viewed as making the Paiute less than fully human. "Whites looked at the Paiute and believed they saw a people who had no fixed habitation, no material culture, no cultivation, no livestock, no homes, and no real claim to humanness" (Langston 2003, 28).

Euro-American views of Paiute relationships with the land were not only biased against a mobile lifestyle, they were also factually incorrect in assuming that native people did not modify the landscape for human use. Paiutes regularly burned riparian areas and wet meadows to stimulate growth of desired plant species and to attract game. Paiutes, especially women, dug for roots and stimulated the growth of edible native plants—a form of cultivation, though not recognized as such by most whites. This alleged lack of industriousness among the Paiute was put forward by whites as proof of Paiute inferiority. In the 1840s, John Frémont, an influential explorer for the US Army Corps of Topographical Engineers, wrote, "Herding together among the bushes, and crouching almost naked over a little sage fire, using their instinct only to procure food,

[Paiute people] may be considered, among human beings, the nearest approach to mere animal creation" (Langston 2003, 31).

Racist and factually inaccurate observations of Native American culture were not incidental: diminution of native people to a perceived subhuman status was a tool used across an expanding American nation in pursuit of manifest destiny to justify conquest, removal, and extermination of native people (Zinn and Arnove 2015). White settlement, military conquest, the taking of native lands, and often extreme brutality toward Paiute peoples in the remote Harney Basin was very much the manifestation of an empire-building political ethos directed by national leadership in Washington, DC, during the second half of the nineteenth century.

Even before large-scale white settlement and conquest, European contacts had brought diseases such as cholera and smallpox that devastated native populations.[5] Further engagement with Euro-Americans brought still more calamity to the Paiute: after several decades of exploration and small-scale white settlement, in 1859 General William S. Harney sent a military expedition to establish a federal presence. Within a year the US Army was hunting down Paiute people, and in 1864 the pro-slavery Oregon Volunteers militia declared full-scale war on all "hostile" Paiutes—after declaring virtually all Paiutes hostile (Langston 2003, 31). After the Civil War, General George Crook received orders to finish the war against the Paiute—and he was soon able to brag that "over half the Indians were killed and the rest reduced to a state of starvation" (Langston 2003, 32).

General Crook then set about negotiating a treaty with the remaining defeated Paiute—an offer he presented as "peace or death" (Burns Paiute Tribe 1995, 3). The treaty, like so many others negotiated with Native Americans across the nation, began promisingly—but the promises were almost immediately broken. A 1,778,560-acre Malheur Indian Reservation (see figure on page 6) was established by executive order on September 12, 1872, to induce the Paiute to settle, adopt farming, and avoid conflicts with whites (Brimlow 1951, 90). Quickly, however, whites began to harass Paiute inside the reservation and murder those who went outside it, even though the Paiute had been promised access to their traditional hunting and gathering sites. The Paiute complained of capricious violence by the government's local "Indian agent," Major William Rinehart, who, in a fit of rage, once ripped the ear off a young Paiute boy he thought had laughed at him—even though the boy did not understand English (Canfield 1983, 110).

The Paiute also complained that Rinehart ignored the terms of the treaty, which included cash payment for labor. In an effort to force the Paiute to adopt agriculture, Rinehart even refused to provide food when access to the Paiute's traditional food sources was closed to them. When the government opened the north shore of Malheur Lake to white settlement in 1877, starvation set in as the Paiute were deprived of a primary source of their staple *wada* (*Suaeda calceoliformis*) seeds. Despite Rinehart's own cruelty, he recognized that even the peaceful Wadatika (seed-eating) Paiute had limits; in 1878, Rinehart complained to his superiors that "stock-men are driving cattle to graze upon the lands of this reservation, and the growing dissatisfaction of the Indians resulting from this is likely to produce future trouble" (Langston 2003, 33).

Rinehart was right that trouble lay ahead. In that same year, the desperation and anger that had been building among Paiute people attempting to survive on Malheur Reservation reached a tipping point. In that year, the neighboring Bannock Tribe from Idaho rebelled and called the Paiute to join them. Some among the generally nonviolent Wadatika band of northern Paiutes reluctantly joined the ill-fated, hopelessly outnumbered rebellion, though by some accounts the majority of Paiutes did not get involved in the fighting.[6] Paiute Chief Egan reportedly stated that

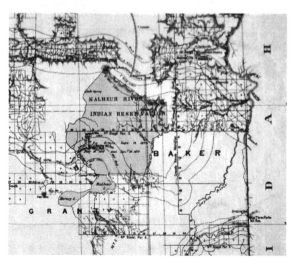

1872 Malheur Indian Reservation. Adapted from original by C. Roesser, General Land Office, Department of the Interior. https://commons.wikimedia.org/w/index.php?curid=25164059

although he knew the Paiute and Bannock had no chance of defeating the white soldiers, with his people facing slow, agonizing death by starvation he might as well die fighting (Langston 2003, p. 174 note 64). Egan's people knew it, too (Burns Paiute Tribe 1995, 5). The uprising was crushed with merciless military force, and the consequences for all Paiute—those who participated and those who did not—were devastating.

Chief Egan was deceived and murdered by members of the neighboring Umatilla Tribe, who—anticipating certain death if they did not cooperate—allied with the US Army. Some Paiute and Bannock escaped into the mountains, but most surrendered and were taken prisoner. Ten years earlier, near the start of Crook's lethal campaign against the Paiute, the tribe's population was estimated at about 2,000 (Burns Paiute Tribe 1995, 5). At the outbreak of the Bannock War, Indian agent William Rinehart estimated the surviving Paiute population at 846 (Brimlow 1951, 104). After the Bannock War, in November 1878, orders were given to remove the 543 living Paiute and Bannock prisoners to the Yakama Indian Reservation in Washington State. About three quarters of the Paiute had been killed in a decade. Those still living faced a terrifying future. On January 6, 1879, shackled men, along with women and children in wagons—many with only blankets for warmth—set out on a 350-mile trek through snowstorms in temperatures near zero (Brimlow 1951, 126). Many died, including an elderly man, two babies, three children, and a mother who had just given birth—their bodies were left frozen along the roadside. More died at the Yakama Reservation, where there was insufficient food and shelter (Canfield 1983, 155). The Yakama were a tribe traditionally hostile to the Paiute, whose language and culture they did not share, and offered little welcome.

When the first white fur trappers and traders entered the Harney Basin in 1826, Peter Skene Ogden of the Hudson's Bay Company observed that he had seen "no Indian nation so numerous as these in all North America" (Brimlow 1951, 10). By the first week of 1879, the Harney Basin was all but emptied of the Paiute people who had thrived among the area's rich ecosystems for more than fourteen thousand years. The remaining traces of Paiute ownership of the land disappeared as well. With almost all local Paiute people killed, starved, imprisoned, and removed—and a handful of others scattered throughout the region as fugitives—Indian agent William Rinehart recommended on August 15, 1879, that the Malheur Reservation be discontinued. In October of that year, it was.

The erasure of the Paiute people from the Harney Basin—their physical presence and their claims to the land—was an essential step that helped to clear the path for major waves of white migration into the Harney Basin in the early 1880s. Even before the Bannock War and the removal of the last Paiute survivors to the Yakama Reservation in 1879, decades of Euro-American warfare against the Paiute created a new kind of landscape—one that appeared deceptively void of human presence. When the young cattle-baron-to-be Pete French arrived in the Blitzen Valley in 1872, for example, he viewed the landscape as empty and free for the taking—lacking any substantial remaining Paiute population to get in the way of his dreams of empire (Langston 2003, 28). The vast French-Glenn Livestock Company would eventually run thirty thousand head of cattle and about six thousand horses and mules in the Blitzen Valley, which was once prime native hunting and gathering territory.[7] One of the largest cattle empires in the American West was built directly on the decimation of the Paiute people and their land rights.

On the former Malheur Indian Reservation, after 1879 cattlemen and settlers rushed in, ending any real possibility of the Paiute people returning to their old lands and ways of life. As of 1887, in accordance with the Dawes Act, the surviving Paiute who had been removed to the Yakama Reservation were allowed to return, each entitled to receive a 160-acre parcel. By then, however, there was almost no land remaining; only 115 agriculturally unproductive parcels were given out.[8] In acres, the land given back to the Paiute was about one percent of the former reservation. For more than four decades, the surviving Wadatika Paiute remained effectively homeless. In 1928, the Egan Land Company donated ten acres of the old Burns city dump to the Paiute. Twenty houses, a community center, a school, and a Catholic church were built. While perhaps better than homelessness, the Paiute's new "home" at the city dump seemed to add insult and indignity to historic injuries against a once-thriving native community.

In 1935, the tribe was able to secure a federal loan to purchase a 771-acre property just north of Burns. However, it was not until 1968 that, after much struggle, the Burns Paiute gained recognition from the Bureau of Indian Affairs, allowing the tribe to declare the 771-acre property plus the "old camp" (dump) property as the Burns Paiute Reservation. The Burns Paiute Reservation remains home base to a reported 410 tribal members as of 2018.[9] In 1969, the tribe finally received payments of as little as $741 per person for the loss of the Malheur Indian Reservation—a figure based on the appraised value of the land in 1879 ($0.28–$0.45 per acre) with no interest after ninety years of inflation (Burns Paiute Tribe 1995, 8).

Although reclaiming substantial ancestral tribal lands appears unlikely for the foreseeable future, federal land stewardship provides a measure of access and protection for once-tribal lands that did not exist when much of the area was controlled by cattle barons. Even today many Paiute consider areas in the Harney Basin far outside the boundaries of the present-day Burns Paiute Reservation to be tribal land, even if not seen as such by most non-Native people. The site of the headquarters of the Malheur National Wildlife Refuge, for example, is rich with archaeological evidence of long-term prehistoric human settlement, inhabited intensively over thousands of years (Aikens and Greenspan 1988). The Malheur Refuge headquarters is also a reburial site for ancestral remains uncovered in other areas where fewer cultural safeguards are available, and it is an important educational site for tribal youth and a place to gather culturally important resources such as reeds for basket-making.

When anti–federal government militants seized the refuge headquarters in 2016, militia promises to "give back" the site to unspecified "rightful owners" deeply distressed the Paiute community. Militants such as Ryan Bundy made it clear that no land would be returned to the Paiutes, stating, "The Native Americans had claim to the land, but they lost that claim."[10] (No acknowledgment was given that these lands were not somehow casually "lost," but taken through murder and exile.) The militants also handled Native American artifacts at the refuge headquarters in ways that Burns Paiute people considered profoundly disrespectful. The return of the refuge headquarters to federal management was a source of great relief.

Ironically, the 2016 militant takeover of the Malheur National Wildlife Refuge increased public awareness of Paiute history and land claims in the region.[11] Former Burns Paiute tribal chair Charlotte Rodrique observed that the US Congress never ratified the treaty that established the Malheur Indian Reservation, so in a legal sense the Paiute never ceded their rights. Nor were they fairly compensated for the land taken from them in the Harney Basin.[12] Nor were most Oregonians familiar with the shameful brutality of the removal of Paiute people to the Yakama Reservation, nor the government-sponsored murder of the Paiute's wise and dignified Chief Egan. If the arc of history bends toward justice, perhaps a fitting outcome of the Malheur takeover would be increased public consciousness that nudges society toward reconciling injustices of the past.

Notes

1   Unnamed Burns Paiute elder, in Louie, M. 1989. "History of the Malheur Paiutes." In *A Lively Little History of Harney County*. Burns, Oregon: Harney County Chamber of Commerce, 5.
2   Burns Paiute Culture and Heritage Director Diane Teeman, personal communication, March 2, 2018.
3   Dennis Jenkins personal communication with author, August 31, 2017.
4   United States History "The Burns Paiute Tribe," accessed May 19, 2018, http://www.u-s-history.com/pages/h1536.html.
5   Ibid.
6   United States History "The Burns Paiute Tribe," accessed May 19, 2018, http://www.u-s-history.com/pages/h1536.html.
7   The Oregon Encyclopedia, a project of the Oregon Historical Society, "John William 'Pete' French (1849-1897)," accessed May 19, 2018, https://oregonencyclopedia.org/articles/john_william_pete_french_1849-1897/#.WwDJ-VMvx24.
8   United States History, "The Burns Paiute Tribe," accessed May 19, 2018, http://www.u-s-history.com/pages/h1536.html.
9   Burns Paiute Tribe homepage, accessed May 20, 2018, https://www.burnspaiute-nsn.gov/.
10 Rebecca Boone, "4,000 artifacts stored at Oregon refuge held by armed group," Associated Press, January 16, 2016, accessed May 19, 2018, https://apnews.com/amp/7e0b0a391bd3425ab5ddb65d2ee7b04f.
11 Kelly House, "Burns Paiutes to Ammon Bundy: you're not the victim," Oregonlive/The Oregonian, February 7, 2016, updated February 23, 2016, accessed May 20, 2018, http://www.oregonlive.com/oregon-standoff/2016/02/burns_paiutes_to_ammon_bundy_y.html.
12 Interview with author, November 17, 2017.

Sage Sparrow Singing

Sage Sparrow singing,

A diamond hard morning,

The radiant sun.

The day came when the white settlers in the Harney Basin and their military escorts began to notice the birds and other wildlife in a scientific, not just a culinary, way. Before there can be conservation, we must know what there is to conserve. What we think of today as scientific study of birds began with observing and collecting what was there. The first significant trove of data from the region came from Charles E. Bendire. Hendrik Herlyn tells us his story.

CHARLES EMIL BENDIRE

Introduced by Hendrik Herlyn

The German Visitors, Part 1

During the second half of the nineteenth century, the exploration of the flora and fauna in the newly acquired western territories of the United States was in full swing. Much of this was driven by officers of the US Army, whose military acumen was paired with a keen interest in natural history, and especially ornithology. Among these early explorers was Captain Charles Emil Bendire who, along with men like Thomas M. Brewer, William C. Cooper, Elliot Coues, Edgar A. Mearns, James C. Merrill and Robert W. Shufeldt, made enormous contributions to our present knowledge of the birds in the western United States.

Born on April 27, 1836, in König im Odenwald, Germany, as the eldest of five children, Karl Emil Bender was initially schooled at home. At the age of twelve, he was sent to a theological seminary near Paris, France, where he spent five years. After being expelled from school for "youthful peccadilloes," he emigrated to America in 1853 at the age of seventeen, accompanied by his brother Wilhelm. Upon his arrival, he anglicized his name to Charles Bendire and enlisted in the US Army, where he initially served in the Medical Corps. He received medals of bravery for his accomplishments in the Civil and Indian Wars and rose to the rank of Captain in 1873. A knee injury forced his retirement from the army in 1886, and in 1890, he was awarded the brevet of Major.

During a leave of absence from the army in 1883, at the request of Professor Spencer F. Baird, Bendire was offered the position of curator of the Department of Zoology at the National Museum in Washington, DC. He continued to hold this position after retiring from the army, and in 1892 published his groundbreaking two-volume work, "Life Histories of North American Birds, with Special Reference to their Breeding Habits and Eggs." He died in 1897 of kidney disease.

Bendire's interest in birds arose early in his military career, while he was stationed in New Mexico and Arizona (where he is credited with the discovery of Bendire's thrasher and the rufous-winged sparrow). Initially, his main focus was collecting eggs (which remained a life-long fascination for him), but he soon began to also collect specimens and study the habits of the birds he encountered. His military tasks included surveys for roads and telegraph lines as well as the exploration of unknown territories, which gave him a unique opportunity to study the avifauna of little-known regions. This included the first military expedition through Death Valley and the study of the deserts of southwestern Nevada. Other postings led him to Louisiana, California, Idaho, Washington, Montana, and two stints in Oregon.

In 1874, the United States Army dispatched Captain Bendire to Camp Harney, an army post at the southwestern edge of the Blue Mountains in Oregon. For the next four years, in addition to fulfilling his military duties, the accomplished naturalist and ornithologist amassed a wealth of information on the birds of this area by collecting numerous specimens and taking copious notes on the occurrence and habits of the birds he encountered there. The results of his studies were published in two papers in the *Proceedings of the Boston Society of Natural History* (Vol. 18, 1875–1876 and Vol. 19, 1876–1878)—the former a list of 79 species observed in the neighborhood of Camp Harney, based on Bendire's correspondence with Thomas M. Brewer, and the latter notes on some of the

birds found in southeastern Oregon, particularly in the vicinity of Camp
Harney, including accounts of 191 species.

Bendire prefaced his species accounts with the following explanation,
which includes a vivid description of an area well-known and dear to
many Oregon birders:

This list is not given as a complete exponent of the avifauna of
Southeastern Oregon. I am well aware that there still remain many
species to be added, particularly of water birds. As far as it goes, it has
been compiled from material now in the hands of Lt. G. R. Bacon,
U. S. A., and from personal observations. Camp Harney (the central
point of my investigations) is located on the southern slope of one of
the western spurs of the Blue Mountains of Oregon, at an altitude
of about 4800 feet in 43° 80' latitude, and 41° 25' longitude, west of
Washington. To the north of the post the country is mountainous and
generally well-timbered with forests of pine, spruce and fir, and groves
of aspens and junipers; in all other directions it is almost destitute of
trees of any size, a few straggling juniper and mountain mahogany
bushes being sparingly distributed over the different mountain ranges.
The highest and most important of these is Steen's [sic] Mountain,
about seventy miles to the south of the post, portions of which range
are covered with snow the year round. Excepting a few warm and fertile river valleys, nearly the whole extent of country is unfit for agriculture. About two-thirds of it is covered with sagebrush and greasewood
wastes, volcanic table-lands, etc., the balance with nutritious grasses,
and well adapted for stock-raising purposes. As a general thing, the
country may be called well watered throughout; a continuous chain
of shallow lakes extends from here to the southwest for more than
two hundred miles, and some of these are from ten to twenty miles
wide and thirty to fifty miles in length. The water in most of them
is brackish, and barely fit to drink. Fine springs, both hot and cold,
are also numerous. The many lakes form a natural highway and con-
venient resting places for the immense hordes of water fowl passing
through here during the spring and fall migrations; they also furnish
safe and undisturbed breeding resorts for many species. The climate,
generally speaking, may be called mild. In the higher mountain valleys

it is almost arctic, ice being formed there even in midsummer; and many species of birds breed there which generally go much farther north for this purpose.

Overall, Bendire's species accounts read much like a current inventory of the birds found in Malheur National Wildlife Refuge and the adjacent areas, describing many of the characteristic marsh, sagebrush, and forest birds we still encounter there today. But he also mentions a few surprises—species that have either disappeared from the area or whose occurrence in Oregon has yet to be properly documented. The former include his accounts of the sharp-tailed grouse and the least bittern, which read as follows:

126. *Pedioecetes columbianus* (Baird). Sharp-tailed Grouse.

Only a moderately common resident, apparently irregularly distributed. In the winter I have seen packs of from one to two hundred in the vicinity of Port Lapwai, Idaho. They frequently roost on the willow bushes along the streams, and I have seen them alight on pine trees on the outskirts of the timber. In the vicinity of Camp Harney they are mostly found in the juniper groves during the cold weather, and the birds live almost exclusively on the berries of these trees. The eggs usually number from eleven to fourteen.

148. *Ardetta exilis* (Gray). Least Bittern.

Apparently rare. I have seen it on but two occasions. It is, however, easily overlooked, and may be rather common.

Bendire mentions two species for which there are no current records in Oregon—black rail and Baird's sparrow. It may be questionable whether he identified these birds correctly, but his records are interesting nonetheless. In Bendire's own words:

152. *Porzana jamaicensis* (Gml.). Little Black Rail.

Seen on two occasions in the swamps near Malheur Lake, where it unquestionably breeds.

47. *Centronyx bairdii* (Baird). Baird's Bunting.

May 24, 1876, I took a nest and four eggs with the parent, which I identified as belonging to this species. The nest was composed externally of old sagebush bark and grasses, and lined with finer materials of the same kind and a few hairs. It was partly concealed under a bunch of tall grass, and found on the flat about five miles below Camp Harney, on the edge of a swampy meadow. The eggs are an elongated oval in shape, ground color a very pale green, three of the eggs marked with irregular spots, lines and blotches of two shades of brown (light and dark, and a few lavender spots. The fourth is blotched throughout with a pale pinkish brown. In the first three eggs the markings are principally about the larger end. Size, .72 × -55, .74 × -56, .71 × .54 and .74 × -54.

Many of Bendire's accounts of the common species he encountered are rather brief and concise, while others go into more detail. To give the reader a better impression of how Bendire saw the birds that surrounded him, I have selected a few examples of species particularly dear to me, whose mention invariably evokes fond memories of the vast marshes and sagebrush steppes of one of my favorite places on earth.

150. *Grus canadensis* (Linn.). Sandhill Crane.
A common summer resident. Breeds abundantly on the lowlands as well as in the highest mountain valleys. Their hoarse cries can be heard almost everywhere where there is any water to be found, and as long as the locality is comparatively quiet, as they are a shy and wary bird. Each pair seems to occupy a certain district during the breeding season, and I have never found two pairs breeding within half a mile of each other. The eggs are usually laid about May 1, and I have never found more than two in a nest. The largest of these measure 4.25 × 2.34 and 4.20 × 2.42 of an inch.

106. *Spheotyto cunicularia* var. *hypogaea* (Bonap.). Burrowing Owl.
A common summer resident, arriving about the end of March. I found it abundant at Fort Lapwai, Idaho, where I obtained a number of their eggs. They preferred hillsides having a southerly exposure. Their holes varied in depth and direction; some were almost straight, others in the shape of a horse shoe, the chamber containing the nest being on a level with the entrance, and in one instance not over a foot

from it, although the whole length of the burrow was at least seven feet. Their nests, of which I examined at least sixteen, consisted of dry cow- or horse-dung, in small pieces, and spread about one and one-half inches thick on the floor of the chamber, which itself was somewhat larger than the passage to it. The usual number of eggs from eight to nine, in one instance ten. The nests were alive with fleas, and the eggs so discolored by them that they resembled more the eggs of the falcons or willow grouse than their natural color.

The birds will remain on their nest and allow themselves to be captured rather than leave the eggs or young. They raise but a brood a season. Their food consists almost exclusively of noxious insects, particularly crickets, and they are exceedingly beneficial to farmers. I do not recollect of having found the remnants of a single small bird in their burrows, but have seen small frogs and mice; their principal food, however, appears to be grasshoppers and crickets. They commence laying about April 25, and work on their burrows at least two weeks before. Only once have I seen one of the birds at work. It pushes and scratches the dirt backwards with its feet.

That they live in harmony with rodents and rattlesnakes is not my opinion. A snake may occasionally enter one of their burrows, but it certainly is never a welcome visitor. I have never found any other living animal in their burrows, and I have examined many. During the breeding season the male utters a call-note resembling that of the European cuckoo (*C. canorus* L.), and scarcely distinguishable from it. Their eggs are not as round, but glossier than owls' eggs generally; some are considerably pointed, a rather unusual shape for eggs of the owl family, and they measure from 1.35 × 1.09 to 1.20 × .98 of an inch. Their color after washing them is pure white.

These accounts by one of the first outside visitors to pay detailed attention to the birds of the region give us a point of departure for much of what came next.

URSULA K. LE GUIN

Desert Lessons

i
In rimrock shade the sudden hiss.
High up on Steens the quick-born storm.
We are at most one step from mortal harm
in this quietness.

ii
Anxieties must change, concern must find
an altered field, before my eye can read
the warning in the dust, and what the cloud
writes on the wind.

iii
Depth beyond blazing depth the stars appear
in utter silence in tremendous night.
A mortal soul in that abyss of light
learns what to fear.

The facts of Malheur slowly became the story of Malheur. The unre-stricted slaughter of the pioneer era was slowly superseded by conser-vation. This transition did not come easily. Visitors began to see what Malheur was, had been, and could be. Among these were the famous writer Dallas Lore Sharp. His descriptions and the work of William L. Finley and Herman T. Bohlman allowed a larger public to know what Malheur meant.

DALLAS LORE SHARP

The Marshes of Malheur

The sedges were full of birds, the waters were full of birds, the tules were full of birds, the skies were full of birds: avocets, stilts, willets, killdeers, coots, phalaropes, rails, tulewrens, yellow-headed black birds, black terns, Forster's terns, Caspian terns, pintail, mallard, cinnamon teal, canvas-back, redhead, and ruddy ducks, Canada geese, night herons, great blue herons, Farallon cormorants, great white pelicans, great glossy ibises, California gulls, eared grebes, Western grebes—clouds of them, acres of them, square miles—*one hundred and forty-three* square miles of them!

I was beside myself at the sight—at the sound—at the thought that such wild life could still be anywhere upon the face of the earth, to say nothing of finding it within the borders of my own land. Here was a page out of the early history of our country—no, an actual area of that wild, unspoiled, unslaughtered country as the Indian knew it, as Lewis and Clark saw it on that first trip across the continent.

The accounts of bird-life in early American writings read to us now like the wildest of wild tales—the air black with flocks of red-winged blackbirds, the marshes white with feeding herons, the woods weighted with roosting pigeons. I have heard my mother tell of being out in a flock of passenger pigeons so vast that the sun was darkened, the birds flying so low that men knocked them down with sticks. As a child I once saw the Maurice River meadows white with egrets, and across the skies of the marshes farther down, unbroken lines of flocking blackbirds that touched opposite sides of the horizon.

That was years ago. I had seen nothing like it since; nor did I ever again expect to see it. I had heard of Malheur Lake, when, some few years ago, the naturalist through whose efforts it was made a federal reservation visited me and told me about it. He even brought photographs of its bird-colonies. But words and pictures gave no conception of the extent of its uncrowded crowds of life. For what could a camera do with one hundred and forty-three square miles of swimming, winging, crying birds?

Lake Malheur Reservation is in the southeastern quarter of Oregon, and is only one of several such wild-life sanctuaries within the borders of that great commonwealth. Indeed, the work being done by Oregon for the protection of wild life seems almost past belief to one used to the small things of the Eastern States. And the work there has but just begun! In 1912 the private game "refuges," where the State Game Warden has entered into contracts with owners of private land, covered an area of 143,789 acres. In addition to these small refuges there are six vast state reservations, set aside forever by the legislature for game and bird protection, covering 1,698,320 acres, or 2,654 square miles, an area more than twice the size of Rhode Island. Besides these state reservations are the four great federal preserves: Three Arch Rocks Reservation, off the coast; Klamath Lake Reservation, lying partly in Oregon and partly in California; Cold Springs Reservation, in Umatilla County, in the northeast; and Lake Malheur Reservation, including the waters and marshlands of Malheur and Harney Lakes, and situated in the midst of protecting sage-brush plains that stretch from the foothills of the Cascades eastward to the cañon of the Snake River at the foot of the Rockies in Idaho.

Separated thus by the deserts from any close encroachment, saved to itself by its own vast size and undrainable, unusable bottoms, and guarded by its federal warden and the scattered ranchers who begin to see its meaning, Lake Malheur Reservation must supply waterfowl enough to restock forever the whole Pacific slope.

For here in the marsh of burr reed and tule, the wild fowl breed as in former times when only the canoe of the Indian plied the lake's shallow waters, when only the wolf and the coyote prowled about its wide, sedgy shores. I saw the coyote still slinking through the sage and salt grass along its borders; I picked up the black obsidian arrowheads in the crusty sand on the edge of the sage plain; and in a canoe I slipped through the green-walled channels of the Blitzen River out into the sea of tule islands amid such a flapping, splashing, clacking, honking multitude as must have risen from the water when the red man's paddle first broke its even surface.

No, not quite such a multitude, for there was no snowy gleaming of egrets in the throngs overhead. The plume-hunter had been before us, and the glory of the lake was gone. That story is one of the tragedies of bird-life, and vividly told in William L. Finley's account of "The Trail of the Plume-Hunter," in the *Atlantic Monthly* for September, 1910. He says, writing of his and Bohlman's journey into the Malheur country in 1908:

> We had hunted where one might think no human being had ever been, but long before we had traveled over these apparently unknown regions, plumers had preceded us. We followed their trails. We camped where they had camped. We had traveled hundreds of miles exploring the haunts where white herons used to live, but up to the summer of 1908 we had not seen a single one of these birds.
>
> This is historic ground for the bird man. In the early seventies the well-known ornithologist, the late Captain Charles Bendire, was sta-tioned at Camp Harney on the southern slope of the Blue Mountains, straight across the valley from where we stood. He gave us the first account of the bird-life in this region. He saw the wonderful sights of the nesting multitudes. He told of the colonies of white herons that lived in the willows along the lower Silvies River. There was the river itself winding across the valley through sage, rye-grass flats, and tule marshes, its trail marked by a growth of willow and alder.

Two days ago we had followed this trail, and searched out these places to photograph the white heron. As we approached the trees, said to be alive with birds, all was silent.

"We're on the wrong trail again," my companion suggested; but pushing through the willows I saw big nests in the trees on both sides of the river. Strange to say, not a single bird! I clambered up to one of the lower nests, and found a rough platform of sticks upon which lay the bleached bones of two herons. I climbed another and another. Each home was a funeral pyre.

"Epidemic?" said my companion.

"Yes, of plume-hunters!" I retorted.

Here was a great cemetery in the silence of the marsh. But one nest was inhabited. A long-eared owl was in possession sitting on five eggs. As we approached, she spread her wings, and left without a sound. Ill-omened creature brooding eggs and bones!

Standing here high above the valley, with my field-glass I picked out the very spot of this great bird-massacre that we had visited.

"I hope we find no more like that," said my companion as he tightened the camera-straps about his shoulders, and started off down the trail toward the lake.

We were both confident that somewhere down in that distant sea of green tules, we could find at least one place where white herons were nesting.

We outfitted for a week's trip, and set out down the spring branch. This time we kept a straight course to the north until we reached the main body of the lake. All day long we hunted and watched birds, lining them with our field-glasses as they flew back and forth over the lake. We saw no signs of white herons.

That day we found a colony where the great blue heron nested. White herons were formerly common here, both species nesting together. Not a single white bird left!

We spent the next four days here and there through the vast extent of tule islands and water, searching and keeping watch all day, trying to find white herons. Late one afternoon we came to a place where another big colony of blue herons was nesting. We had been seeking this place. Malheur Lake is divided in several parts by the long lines of tule islands. We were in the northern part. The colony was on two long tule islands that lined up with Pine Knob and the east end of Wright's Point. On the north end is a big canebrake.

We sat in the boat at the edge of the canebrake, and watched the big birds as they sailed over, dropped in, and departed. We were tired from the long day's search: but hidden in the end of this canebrake a hunter had had his blind, ten years before.

That summer of 1898 was eventful in white-heron history here on Malheur Lake. Early in the season two men had arrived at Narrows, bought lumber, and built a flat-bottom, double-ended boat. They set out from Narrows with a small outfit. They fought mosquitoes day and night as we had; they drank the alkali water; they slept in the boat or on muskrat house while they hunted up and down the waters of the lake and the tule islands. They saw the great flocks of white pelicans, cormorants, terns, gulls, grebes, and other birds. They saw the white herons in slow, stately flight wherever they went, but it was not till after several days that they located the big colony here on the island by the canebrake, the greatest colony they had ever seen. What a sight it must have been, thousands of these birds, dazzling white in the sun, coming and going from the feeding-grounds, and hovering over their homes!

On all sides were the homes, built up a foot or two from the surface, each having three or four frowsy-headed youngsters or as many eggs. At each end of the colony a plumer sat hidden in his blind. At the first crack of the gun, a great snow bird tumbled headlong near its own nest. As the shot echoed across the lake, it sounded the doom of the heron colony. Terror-stricken, on every side white wings flapped, till the air was completely filled. Shot followed shot unremittingly as the minutes passed into hours. Still the heron mothers came to hover over this scene of death and destruction. Mother-love was but the lure to slaughter.

By two o'clock in the afternoon, the day's shoot ended. It took the rest of the day for the hunters to collect the dead and take the plumes. Stripping the plumes is rapid work. It takes but the slash of the knife across the middle of the back, a cut down each side, and a swift jerk.

Long after dark the plumers heard the steady quacking clatter of young herons crying to be fed. Far into the night, hoarse croaks sounded over the still lake, greetings of those birds that had spent the day fishing in distant swamps. It argued good shooting again for the morrow.

The second day was a repetition of the first. Heron numbers thinned rapidly. Here on these two islands, the plumers harvested a crop that yielded twelve hundred dollars in a day and a half. They collected a load of plumes worth their weight in gold. Were the California days of '49 much better?

Malheur has seen many such massacres, but none so great as that. Little did we know of these facts as we sat watching the blue herons coming and going, expecting to find at least a few white herons somewhere about the locality.

After hunting for seven days we returned to camp for more provisions, and set out to visit another part of the lake. This time we stayed out for nine days, and saw—two white herons! At the time we thought these must be part of a group that nested somewhere about the lake; yet more likely they were a single stray bird that came our way twice. I am satisfied that of the thousands of white herons formerly nesting on Malheur, not a single pair of birds is left.

It may have been *two* birds that they saw and not one. For he has not told all of the story yet; how in the summer of 1912 he received a telegram saying white herons (the American egret) had been seen passing over the marshes of Malheur; nor how we set out from Portland for Burns; nor how, away off on an island in the alkali water of Silver Lake, some fifty miles in the desert from Malheur, we found the birds—a colony of a dozen pairs, numbering with the young about twenty-eight birds all told; nor how—

But that is for him to tell, if he will. For if the egret is ever again seen flying over the inland waters of the Pacific coast, it will be due to William L. Finley, to his discovery of the slaughter on his trip to Malheur in 1908, and to his efforts which made Malheur a wild-bird reservation.

But was it, we wonder, one bird or two that he saw winging over the lake in 1908? If two birds, were they male and female? And were they the last two? And is this small colony, which we discovered four years later in Silver Lake, the seed of that last solitary pair? Could it have been that the race was so nearly cut off in all this part of the world? And does it mean that slowly now, with the new protection of these better times, the egret will come back to the willows along the Silvies and at Clear Lake, and to the islands in the canebrake of the Malheur?

I think so. In the willows of Silver Lake, I counted twenty-eight birds. These are enough if they are given a chance. The life of the species, however, does not hang upon this perilously slender thread. Along the Gulf and Southern Atlantic States, and in the Middle West, small colonies are reported as surviving, mere handfuls, where the plume-hunter found immense rookeries. Bird-lovers the world over are watching these remnants with intense concern. Nowhere were the herons as nearly wiped out, it appears, as in Oregon; and nowhere will their escape and ultimate restoration seem more of a miracle.

But desert and marsh and even my little woodlot are full of miracles. The ways of Nature are not past finding out; she does not move so mysteriously as amazingly, her wonders to perform. She could not restore the American egret without a pair to work with. She never could use crows for the purpose. But given the pair of birds, then the loaves and fishes become snowy, winged things, gleaming above the marsh by thousands, and decked in bridal dress of surpassingly lovely plumes.

While here on Malheur I witnessed a sight among the grebes, that gave me further reason for my faith in the resources of Nature, open as the happening may be to a contrary interpretation.

On the day of our arrival at the town of Burns, the wardens of Malheur met us with the report of a new grebe colony (these birds had also nearly been exterminated by the plume-hunter), which they had discovered only the day before off in the lake. We had ridden across the desert that afternoon in the teeth of a stiff wind, and the wardens, anxious to show us the new colony, were greatly concerned for fear that this wind might wreck the nests exposed to its sweep across the wide level of the lake.

For it was nesting-time and the colony had built far out on the open water in a close, continuous line a mile long and three hundred yards wide—a community of twenty-four hundred floating nests.

The figures are true. The wardens actually staked off the colony, measured it, and literally counted the nests. I paddled along its length myself, and while I did not count, I did believe their figures.

It was to visit this colony of grebes that we wound our way through the narrow turnings of the Blitzen River out into the wider maze of the vast lake, where there was nothing to be seen but water and tules—and birds, myriads of birds. But the wardens had blazed a trail by tying the tule-tops together into big knots, which we could see from island to island ahead of us as we paddled along.

This was on Monday. It was on Thursday the week before that the wardens had found the colony; and now, as we came out of the mouth of the Blitzen, we ran straight into a grebe colony of over a hundred nests that was not there at all four days before. One of the wardens, who was in the canoe with us, thought we must be off the course. But here were his knots in the tules. The nests had been built, all of them, since Thursday, and most of them were already with eggs.

There must be some mistake, I thought, and turned to watching the birds; for it was not the nests that interested me half so much as the anxiety of the grebes at discovering us. Every one began hurriedly pulling the wet tule stems and milfoil of the nest over her eggs to hide them before we should come up, working against her fears, and at the risk of her life, to save her eggs—to protect the seed of the race!

A racial instinct, you say, only a race act, every bird doing as every other bird did that had eggs. True, but here, as with the murres on Three-Arch Rocks, there was plainly individual action, deep individual concern, the mother feeling, holding some of the birds to their duty long after others had taken wing in fright.

To rob the animals of individuality—to reduce them to automata, acting mechanically according to inherited race instincts, is to reduce all life to grass and the grass almost to hay.

> Through primrose tufts, in that green bower,
> The periwinkle trailed its wreaths,
> And 'tis my faith that every flower
> Enjoys the air it breathes.

And 'tis my further faith that every bird and animal and insect enjoys the air it breathes, and loves and hates and woos and fights and suffers, not in the same degree, but somewhat after the manner of humans.

To her fair works did Nature link
The human soul that through me ran. [Wordsworth]

I, too, am an automaton, a wheel in a great race-machine. I do certain things because the race has done them and continues to do them. Perhaps I have never done anything that the race has not done. Perhaps I am my whole race. Perhaps I have been in my development, since I was conceived, all the races down to the single-celled amoeba. Yet I am; and the race is; but as for the race, I can say, "Go to!"

So the individual grebe is. The sight of these hundred feverishly pulling down the walls of their nests to cover their eggs was a very human sight, poignant, personal, and not the mechanics of race instinct at all.

The grebe builds a floating nest out in the open water. All over the bottom of the clear lake, which averages about four feet in depth, grew the long, trailing, mosslike water milfoil, its whorled leaves and purple stems giving a faint glow of color to the water as we looked down into it. The grebes dive to the bottom and drag up this milfoil into heaps, or cocks, about six feet across on the bottom. The cocks are barely able to float their tops above the surface. Upon the very peak of this cock they hollow out a nest about the size of a man's hat, building up the walls with dead tule stems until the eggs rest just out of the water, though many of them are partly submerged. The nests are usually so close together that their wide bases touch below, but otherwise they are entirely unanchored and at the mercy of wind and wave.

This was the cause of the warden's anxiety, and, halting only long enough to count the new nests and get some photographs at the mouth of the river, we pushed on up the lake.

I shall try to describe that trip sometime—the long lines of white water kicked up by the rising birds; the clapping of wings, the splashing of feet; the tule islands trodden flat by the rookeries of young gulls and pelicans and cormorants; the diving of the grebes about us; the soaring of the majestic pelicans far above us—but not any of that now.

We had paddled for an hour or two when on the water in the distance appeared a wide wash of pink, as if the clouds of a sunset were reflected there. It was the purple of the milfoil in the nests of the great grebe colony. We quickened our stroke, and as we drew nearer, marveling at the extent of it, we were struck with the silence at our coming and the absence of birds in the nests. A few were on wing; a few were seen covering their eggs; that was all. There was not clangor of the crowd, no diving multitude about us—but such a sight of destruction as I hope never again to see!

Of the twenty-four hundred nests not three hundred were left. Tossed and torn, the nests had been driven by the high waves and the strong wind back upon themselves, in some places several deep, their pale white eggs by thousands scattered through the tangled debris or floating free in the water.

The rookery was an utter wreck. The birds, with the exception of a few pairs, had abandoned it—had gone, some hundred pairs of them, down to the mouth of the Blitzen and there started the new colony which we had encountered coming out.

I don't know which impressed me more—the fearful loss and waste of life here, or the thought of that quick recovery at the mouth of the Blitzen.

The birds had shown no judgment in choosing this place for their rookery. No more exposed position could have been found in the entire lake. The colony had acted blindly, stupidly; had learned nothing as a colony in their million ages of nest-building, nor ever shall learn. But how swift to begin again! How fertile in resource! How absolute to command! With the nest done, the season's clutch of eggs laid, and incubation started, to see it all destroyed, and in less than a week to have built again and to have summoned the secret forces of life with new eggs for the new nests!

Can a man be born when he is old? No, because there is not a need for such rebirth. But if there were need, if that were the only way of preserving the race, the thing would be done.

The autumn winds strip my trees of their withered leaves, and the buds swell and leaf out again in the spring. That is the natural cycle. There is nothing mysterious about that. The caterpillars stripped them of their green leaves in July. The naked things shrank and shuddered in the burning heat, the sap standing still in their veins. Then, instantly laying hold with their manifold fingers on the subtile threads of life, they wove and fashioned and put on a new mantle, a miracle, that the span of the summer might be crossed, and the seed carried over for another spring.

It was so with the grebes. It is so with all life—each living thing a multitude, each individual its whole race latent—potent if need be.

A bare handful of the former myriads of the white herons, or egrets, are left on Malheur. I hope to make the trip again from Bend to Burns, and from Burns down to Malheur Reservation, in order to see the gleaming, shimmering flocks of the snowy creatures that I am sure shall be passing to and from their island rookeries in the cane and tules at the head of the marshy lake.

C.E.S. WOOD

excerpt from
Poet in the Desert

The little rivers run away from the rugged Titans who are wrapped
    in cloaks of azure.
They steal out from the mountains into the bosom of the Desert;
And the willows follow after them, waving their hands, calling that
    they not run so fast away.
The river builds a safe fortress where the birds hide and the ante-
    lopes come for shelter.
The carpet is a weaving of sweet grasses;
But at last the impatient life-givers marry
The marshes which in the Springtime are green with tule-rush and
    in autumn copper-red;
Vast sanctuaries for the herons, ducks, pelicans and plover.
Here breed the stately cranes which in the fading year mount high
    to the cloudless heavens and circle about calling for the South-
    land.
Who is their monitor? Who is their pilot?

PART 2

The Meaning of Refuge

What is a wildlife refuge? It is what it can be made to be. In the early years of Malheur National Wildlife Refuge, little could be made of a dry valley and an empty lake. A combination of Depression prices, Congressional action, and waters from the sky brought the refuge to life. Timing is everything. Ira Gabrielson was a young biologist then. He would rise to become the first head of the US Fish and Wildlife Service. He was there at the beginning of the resurrection of Malheur.

IRA N. GABRIELSON

Malheur Then and Now

I first saw Malheur Lake in Oregon as a young federal biologist nearly a half-century ago, and the impression of that first visit is one of my most vivid memories. Since that time I have seen many spectacular concentrations of wildlife in various parts of the world, but nothing that I have seen since has dimmed the almost physical impact that the sight of Malheur Marsh made upon me as I stood breathless on a grassy ridge called Cole Island on a late summer morning. A sea of marsh vegetation, broken only by occasional patches of open water and a few low dunes, stretched almost endlessly from horizon to horizon. There had been more than usual precipitation that summer, and Malheur Lake was well filled with water; farther beyond, Mud Lake shimmered in the sunlight; and there even was water in Harney Lake, which usually was reduced to a broad, white salt flat by late summer.

In, over, and through this sea of bulrushes, arrowhead, and pondweed moved the most awe-inspiring concentration of birdlife that I had ever seen. Squadrons of white pelicans, so densely crowded that they appeared from a distance as shifting banks of snow, fished in the open water. Fleets of Canada geese cruised the lakes, ignoring the American coots and the ducks of a dozen species that thronged about their flanks. Great blue herons and common egrets stalked in stately silence among the rushes.

In the intervening space, the flats were covered with smaller herons, American avocets, willets, black-necked stilts, plovers, and sandpipers loafing, walking, running, or rising in flashing clouds to alight on a better hunting ground a few rods beyond. This moving, pulsing mass of life extended far beyond the range of my binoculars—and these were only the forerunners of the autumn migration!

Once the impact of the sight had subsided enough to permit detailed observation, the number of species that could be identified from a single spot was amazing. In later years, I have seen greater concentrations of birdlife in the nesting rookeries of colonial birds throughout North America, but nowhere in any one spot have I identified anything like the variety of birds that was present upon that first trip to Malheur.

Soon after my first visit, Malheur began to decline, although it remained a waterfowl paradise until the early 1920s. Malheur Lake had been set aside by Theodore Roosevelt as a national wildlife refuge in 1908, making it one of the oldest refuges in North America; but the early reservation had failed to include the water rights above the lake. Malheur and Harney Lakes form the sump for a great watershed, including the south slope of the Blue Mountains and the west slope of the Steens. When irrigation developed in the Harney Valley, the water in Silvies River, which rises in the Blue Mountains, never reached the lake in drier years. When similar developments in the Blitzen Valley diverted the flow from the Steens Mountains, the fate of Malheur Lake seemed sealed.

By 1926, Malheur had become almost a desert, and a few years later, in the late summer, one could drive an automobile anywhere over the exposed lake bottom. Little remained of what, a decade before, had been one of the greatest wildlife spectacles to be seen in America since the passing of the bison migrations. Only remnants could be found of the nesting concentrations, and the waterfowl and shorebirds that had once thronged its marshlands now passed over it without stopping on their journeys north and south.

Malheur appeared to be gone, but it was not forgotten. In Oregon, a small group of dedicated conservationists and naturalists fought long and hard to obtain funds to restore it. Negotiations with the landowners who controlled the water rights along the Blitzen and the Silvies made little progress. Land prices were prohibitive, and the legal problems involved were insurmountable for any small local group.

Hope for restoration of Malheur Lake came from an unwelcome source. The Great Depression of the early 1930s spelled disaster for many Americans, but it was responsible for making possible the restoration of Malheur Lake. Land prices suddenly declined sharply. At the same time, Jay N. ("Ding") Darling was appointed chief of the Bureau of Biological Survey and arrived in Washington bursting with enthusiasm for saving waterfowl by extending the national wildlife refuge system. Moreover, he had wrangled from a not-too-sympathetic administration and Congress the largest appropriation for wildlife ever made up to that time for waterfowl in America.

Those of us in the service who knew Malheur were unanimous in recommending that the water rights, controlled by the P Ranch in the Blitzen Valley, be given top priority in Ding's far-reaching land acquisition program. I still was in Oregon in the fall of 1934 when a telegram reached me from Darling stating, in effect: "The P Ranch is ours. Turn the water back into the lake." It was one of the most welcome messages I have ever received.

Restoration began as soon as the water began to flow. The eastern third of the lake was bisected by an eleven-mile dike to retain the returning water, but provisions were made to reflood the entire lake bed as more water became available. Ponds, sloughs, and channels were created in the Blitzen Valley—a long, narrow gorge hemmed in by basalt cliffs—and this area, with the Double O Ranch on Silver Creek, acquired in a later purchase, became one of the most important waterfowl production units of the region.

I saw Malheur Lake die and saw it reborn, and it remains one of my favorite spots in an increasingly complex world. I visit it as often as opportunity permits. Many times, I have stood for hours at the site of the present headquarters, watching the birds moving about, all the while drinking in the beauty of the endless vista of marsh.

The heart of the Malheur National Wildlife Refuge was, and still is, Malheur Lake. In the fall it becomes the feeding and concentration area for most of the water birds produced in the entire Harney Basin, and later it becomes a great aquatic marshaling yard for southbound migrants.

Harney Lake, the sink for the basin, is dry much of the time, and frequently appears as a broad salt flat rimmed with sparsely vegetated dunes. It is one place in eastern Oregon where the snowy plover may be found with some certainty, although even there it is not a common bird. On Malheur Lake the concentrations of herons, pelicans, cormorants, grebes, ducks, geese, and shorebirds reach incredible proportions.

The Blitzen Valley and the Double O Ranch are not only the most important waterfowl nesting grounds but they also offer the greatest possibility for seeing a variety of birds within a limited area. Along the spectacular rim-rock cliffs, great horned owls, prairie falcons, and (western) red-tailed hawks nest regularly. On occasions, I have seen pairs of Canada geese incongruously nesting far above the valley floor on the cliffs. One pair nested precariously for several years between a pair of horned owls and a pair of red-tailed hawks. The gander, standing guard above the nest, was the most conspicuous bird in the landscape.

The fact that greasewood, rabbitbrush, and sagebrush grow from the base of the rim rock to the edge of the marsh provides a fascinating variety of habitat. By turning 180 degrees, one can watch nesting cranes, geese, ducks, avocets, stilts, and other waterfowl and shorebirds on one side and sage thrashers, Brewer's sparrows, and Swainson's hawks on the other. There are relatively few places where one can see, from the same spot, long-billed marsh wrens, rock wrens, and, less frequently, cañon wrens without moving a step.

With the approach of fall, northern migrants begin swelling the numbers of birds present, and within weeks the panorama of life reaches a peak. Malheur is a regular gathering spot for snow and white-fronted geese, and long files of whistling swans pitch into the open water to feed and rest before moving south. Shorebirds, ducks, and other waterfowl from the northern nesting grounds become prominent players in a spectacular autumnal show whose cast of characters and performance vary from one day to the next.

Malheur also offers a wide variety of mammalian life, especially in the Blitzen Valley. Mule deer are common and unafraid of the observer; pronghorn antelope are conspicuous residents of the more open and drier areas; coyotes are often seen; and the beavers' engineering activities are much in evidence. These industrious rodents may often be seen in the early morning and late afternoon. Black-tailed jackrabbits and cottontails are abundant in some years and are present in numbers at all times.

Many small desert rodents, including chipmunks, ground squirrels, kangaroo rats, and a number of species of mice also are to be seen. If one turns the lights of his automobile across and area laced with tracks, he is likely to see many of these nocturnal creatures. The kangaroo rat is the most interesting of all. Its comical antics often have furnished me with a more acceptable desert substitute for a feature television show.

Malheur today holds within its boundaries every species of bird that was nesting there on my first visit. Some species may be even more abundant now than they were at that time, and a well-organized management program is increasing its value to wildlife each year.

In contrast to Malheur, Lower Klamath Lake, when I first viewed it, was a pitiful remnant of its former magnificence, and its companion, Tule Lake, was rapidly approaching that condition. The Bureau of Reclamation, by diverting the waters of the Klamath Marsh, had virtually destroyed its productivity as a wildlife area. Tule Lake, the old sump of Lost River, was being treated similarly, but enough return-flow irrigation water reached it to maintain a sizable area of permanent marsh. Later, as more land was brought under irrigation, the return flow of life-giving water increased, and Tule Lake was restored to its present size. It became a national wildlife refuge in 1928.

Eventually, so much water was flowing back into Tule Lake that the six thousand acres diked off by the US Fish and Wildlife Service were unable to contain it. When the dike broke and several thousand acres of cropland were flooded, the surplus waters were diverted through a tunnel, built by the Bureau of Reclamation, into Lower Klamath Lake, and the Fish and Wildlife Service constructed a dike along the Oregon-California boundary to impound the water on the bottom of Lower Klamath. Through this interservice cooperation, both Tule and Lower Klamath Marshes were partially restored to their original magnificence.

There are five national wildlife refuges in the Klamath Basin. All of them are worth visiting; but the Tule (37,000 acres) and Klamath (22,800 acres) areas, while small compared to their original size, still furnish food and living space to the most spectacular duck and goose concentrations to be found on this continent. From late September until freezing weather, these two refuges play host to "millions" of birds.

One of my favorite pastimes while in Oregon was to climb well up the talus slope of the rim behind what is now the Tule Lake headquarters and watch the multitude of birds coming and going. There were similar vantage points on the present Klamath refuges, and either offers a vivid autumnal picture that is beyond my ability to describe.

Once, when instructed to estimate the number of birds present on Tule Lake, I watched for hours trying vainly to find some formula with which to make even a rough estimate of the number of ducks within the range of my binoculars. My report that there was a "hell of a lot of ducks" failed to satisfy those sponsoring the estimate, and I was instructed to go back and try again. I did, only to find even more birds, if that were possible. My second effort didn't give me a more accurate estimate, but I did submit a figure that was pulled completely out of the air. Since I heard no more about it, the powers were either satisfied or gave it up as a bad job.

The Klamath Basin refuges furnish food for the migrant hordes but, equally important, they hold birds out of the rice fields in the Sacramento and San Joaquin Valleys of California until the harvest is well along. If for any reason, these areas ever cease to be available to birds, the crop depredation problem in the valleys to the south will become disastrous.

This is not their only value, however, for all refuges in the basin contain spectacular colonies of breeding birds. On these areas in May and June are to be found colonies of white pelicans, herons, egrets, cormorants, gulls, terns, and grebes. Avocets, stilts, Wilson's phalaropes, and a great variety of other birds are also common nesters.

Upper Klamath and the Klamath Refuge are both bordered, to some extent, by coniferous forests that attract additional arboreal species of birds to the basin refuge. Among the more interesting are the white-headed woodpecker, black-backed three-toed woodpecker, and Williamson's sapsucker, all of which I have seen on the Upper Klamath.

All of these refuges provide nesting habitat for Canada geese and many ducks, the most common of which are the mallard, gadwall, redhead, cinnamon teal, and ruddy duck. The refuges in the Klamath Basin and the Malheur gave me my first opportunity to see really big marshes. Looking back over the seventeen years in which these areas were within the district assigned to me by the US Bureau of Biological Survey, there were so many new experiences that a mere catalogue of them would fill many pages.

My first golden eagle nest was on a rim close to Malheur. Incidentally, it was the only one I ever found that could be reached without strenuous effort, and it afforded a real opportunity to become acquainted with this splendid species.

As a boy, I saw each spring the movements of sandhill cranes through western Iowa. Their "quiver dance" in the fields and sonorous calls, as they circled slowly high overhead, were spectacular, but it remained for Malheur to give me the first sight of a crane nest and the first chance to watch the spindle-legged youngsters after they hatched.

Similarly, I found my first western and eared grebe nests at Malheur, and there I first sighted a common egret's nest. The Klamath area likewise showed me my first Canada goose, redhead, and cinnamon teal nests. Willets, American avocets, black-necked stilts, long-billed curlews, and common snipe were among the shorebirds whose nests and courtship performances I first witnessed in one of these basins.

It would be a serious omission if I failed to mention the great colonies of pelicans, California and ring-billed gulls, and Caspian and Forster's terns whose nests are still found here.

The opportunities for serious bird students to add to present ornithological knowledge are almost unlimited on these refuges, and while it is true that the Fish and Wildlife Service is carrying on considerable biological work, the men assigned to these studies would be the first to admit that they have not been able to avail themselves of existing opportunities. The chance to study behavior, life histories, population dynamics, and interrelationships between species, to mention only a few possibilities, are endless.

It always has been one of my regrets that these areas became refuges staffed with biologists only after I was no longer a field biologist and had become deeply entangled in administrative details.

If I were a young biologist again, nothing would suit me better than to be able to live and work with the abundant wildlife on those refuges. It would make little difference whether the assignment was to study the big and showy water birds or some of the shy and obscure small desert birds about which so little is known; it is one opportunity that I still wish had been my lot.

In this section, individual narratives by the late Tom McAllister and Dave Marshall, supplemented by a transcription of a joint presentation that they gave in 2005, provide a multi-angled look at the formative years of Malheur as we know it today. The teenage Tom McAllister arrives at Malheur from Portland during World War II, learning by experience what really happens on a wildlife refuge. His friend Dave Marshall also visits the refuge as a teenager before beginning his career as a wildlife biologist. The spectral presence of the war takes these young men into the Navy and the Army Air Force, respectively—but they return to the magnet of Malheur. Tom and Dave take us on a tour of the refuge as John Scharff knew it and ran it, a unique personal fiefdom among refuges, and one that worked in its time and place.

TOM MCALLISTER

My Summer in Paradise

Going on sixteen with a passion for birding, my dream destination was Malheur National Wildlife Refuge. But it was 1942 with our nation engulfed in war. That meant rationing and limited travel.

My dad, a Portland dentist who encouraged my range of outdoor interests, had a plan. His patients included Harney County ranch families who made annual trips to Portland for medical-dental needs and major shopping, usually prior to Christmas. They stayed downtown on Broadway at the Imperial Hotel (now the boutique Vintage Plaza on the National Historic Register).

Included was a Mrs. MacDonald who operated Frenchglen Hotel with her son Finley and daughter Catherine. This was the waypoint for cattle and sheep men, cinnabar (mercury ore) prospectors, and business travelers headed south from Burns into Nevada. Dad simply exchanged the MacDonalds' dental bill for my time at Malheur Refuge.

I was enroute by Trailways Bus June 25th on the Portland to Boise run via Maupin, Bend, and Burns in unseasonable (for east of the Cascades) continuous downpour. The bus rolled in after midnight and Mrs. MacDonald met me on arrival at the town watering hole, the old Arrowhead Hotel. We were away in a pickup with a local handyman driver named Cliff.

Not a light shone in the sixty-five miles to Frenchglen. There was then no Rural Electrification Administration to supply power to the hinterlands. We sped alone that night, dead center over loose gravel, washboard, and muddied reaches and never let up for dips, except when a deer loomed along the shoulder. I didn't know how fast we drove as the car's panel lights were out.

This west side city kid was impressed and wide awake. The heady aroma of wet sage and juniper filled the drizzly night, and birding was there in the headlight beams. On reaching The Narrows the moon appeared briefly and fishing great egret, snowy egret, and black-crowned nightheron were visible at the road edge. Caught in the headlights were ghostly great horned owls that swept over the road,

Burrowing owls with glowing eyes standing by their burrows and ruby-eyed poorwills. There was the tire thump from black-tailed jackrabbits that zigged when they should have zagged. The number of rabbits was astounding. Kangaroo mice bounced over the road and a pup coyote jumped aside. We arrived in Frenchglen at 3 a.m.

It continued raining my first day, so with mud everywhere I stuck close and visited the barn to get acquainted with the milk cow and the horses, Spud, Popeye, and the mare Flaxy with her wobbly new filly. Barn swallows shared the chicken house, and there was a pig pen and garden. This bungalow-style little ranch hotel was partly food sufficient. In the garage the Say's phoebe had an occupied nest of mud and straw stuck with no visible support against a roof rafter. Before dinner I rode Spud, who was one-eyed, into the meadow and flushed my first gadwall.

The only hotel guests were botanists Dr. Morton E. Peck of Willamette University and his wife Terrece. His *Manual of the Higher Plants of Oregon* (1941) remains a definitive work. I joined the Pecks on subsequent collecting trips, packed plant presses, and got a botany introduction. While plant collecting in the Jackass Mountains I found my first Brewer's sparrow on its nest, well concealed three feet off the ground in the center of a sage bush. The fine grass nest was lined with horse hairs and held four pale blue-green eggs speckled brown on the large end. Sage sparrows were so wary they kept running through light and shadow under the shrubs, so it took time for an identification. My first Swainson's hawk proved notable for buteos as it was seen the most frequently.

Sharp youthful vision for new sparrows was somewhat enhanced with a pair of French 4× field glasses. Binoculars were rare and too expensive. I made do for photographs with a Brownie box camera. As for birding references our single best field guide at that time was *Birds of the Pacific States* by Ralph Hoffman. I still use this well-worn book given to me in 1941 on my birthday by boyhood birding companions David Marshall and Bill Telfer. This early guide is so satisfying both for its superb Allan Brooks pen and ink drawings and Hoffman's informative morsels of information that today's guides overall lack.

Best of all on the Jackass Mountains was the startling roar of greater sage-grouse flushing from tall sage. The Pecks introduced me to a long-stem fleshy onion that had a tasty root and dark blue flower cluster. Old-timer Walt Riddle, who with his brother homesteaded on the upper Blitzen River (now a BLM historic site), came off the mountain with his buckboard and team. Riddle didn't look like he had a bean in his jeans, but family from Burns drove out with his Cadillac to retrieve him. Riddle had great stories about Peter French and the Paiute Indians.

My first day I also checked out Bradeen Bros. General Store next to the hotel. It had everything of necessity from reading glasses and blanket pins to kerosene lamps, a hundred-pound sack of oats for $1.60 or fifty pounds of stock salt for seventy-five cents. For best use of the limited store space, hardware was suspended from ceiling hooks. Customers looked up and cut down with their pocket knife. The store accepted pairs of jackrabbit ears strung on wire hoops for the five-cent bounty delivered at the county court. The store kept one-half cent for handling.

At boarding house–style meals we had passing buckaroos and sheep-herders and Basque prospectors from Winnemucca. The German U-boats cut off America's source of mercury in Spain and South Africa, so the Steens and Pueblo Mountains were strategic mineral sites. High school boys working at Swift and Company's Roaring Springs Ranch came down from Catlow Valley for a Mrs. MacDonald meal. Coin of the realm in those times was one silver dollar dropped into a cut glass bowl on the dinner table.

A Chicago windmill hooked to a series of batteries generated enough power to turn the lights on briefly at night, power the washing machine, and listen to the radio. Then sandhill crane, common nighthawk, poorwill, snipe, coyote, and rustling poplar leaf sounds prevailed as we sat in the dark on the screened porch.

June 27 was my white-throated swift day. Finley and I had the wood gathering chore, which meant driving a 1932 International flatbed we called "Leaping Lena." That's what it did as we worked upward over a dim bulb track into the junipers in compound low gear. Screaming over the rim above Catlow Valley was a swarm of the very swifts I had my heart set on finding. We also hunted rabbits Finley style. While one drove in turn the other on the truck bed leaned flat over the cab top and struck it to alert the driver to brake for a .22 rifle shot at a flushed jackrabbit.

That evening we fished Blitzen River and caught a seventeen-inch redside breakfast trout. There was a colony of cliff swallows at the diversion dam, the mosquitoes were voracious, and I picked five ticks from my hide. My diary notes there were no mosquitoes by the swallow colony, and, "best of all I saw a gray catbird in the willows near the Blitzen bridge," another of so many firsts to come. Mrs. MacDonald along with the other women on the far-flung ranches made up picnic hampers before everyone headed that night after chores to a dance and midnight supper at The Narrows Schoolhouse. Folks arrived about ten or eleven, danced the night away, and headed home with sunup.

On June 28 Finley and I were on a wood run onto Steens Mountain with time aside for trout fishing in Fish Creek, but we lost that track and ended back on the Blitzen. But I saw my first mountain bluebirds. That electric blue was dramatic. Compared to white-crowned sparrows on my west side home turf these Steens white-crowns sang with a quick wheezy cadence. There was lots of high snow after the late storms, and a full moon over the Steens crest gave the mountain a ghostly white glow.

June 29 I rode Spud to Catlow Valley; he went up at a plod and homeward at a brisk trot. Took a bath in a hot springs, another first, near the Charlie Barnes Ranch. This night resonated with the guttural rolling calls of sandhill cranes aroused by the fullness of the moon.

On June 30 I crossed the wet meadows to the P Ranch. Saw sandhill pairs with their russet colts at close range. Climbed the CCC-built refuge lookout tower, a favored roost for turkey vultures, and had an overview of Blitzen Valley. Visited at Bradeens with two old-sod Irish sheepherders, the Calahans. Mosquitoes terrible while feeding the pigs that evening.

On July 1 I rose at 4:30 a.m. with a dawn chorus led by Bullock's orioles just outside my window. Walked about two miles north from French-glen, brushing and smacking skeeters all the way, while listening to tule (marsh) wren, rock wren, sora, mourning dove, red-winged blackbird, and incessant killdeer pairs that had one nesting territory after another along the gravel road.

When I returned for breakfast I learned that Refuge Manager John Scharff knew about the boy from the Audubon Society. He arranged with Mrs. MacDonald for me to meet biologist Ray Sooter at the P Ranch. She packed me a lunch and I rode my horse to meet Sooter, who drove us to the assembly point on Boca Lake where we would round up and band Western Canada geese, now in their brief flightless period.

There I first met Scharff and Ray Erickson from Iowa State University, who was completing a master's degree on nesting canvasback in the Great Basin. Malheur Refuge then had some three hundred nesting canvasback. There were seven of us on the goose drive with three boats and a canoe. I was directed to walk the lake margin and pace the flotilla toward an embayment where wing nets led into a banding enclosure. There was lots of hollering, can banging, and oar smacking to move those agitated geese. Western grebe calls added to the din. In haste and excitement I left hat and canteen at the hotel, so I stopped to cool down on that long goose drive. I crouched under a shading rock overhang on the lake edge, took off my boots, and soaked my feet. I started again with a cooling wet shirt, pants, and bandanna. What a relief!

Banding geese at Malheur, 1942.

Some 900 geese started toward the trap, about 400 arrived and half by sheer weight pushed the fencing over, and 211 remained in the outer holding pocket. They were pushed in small groups into the innermost pocket where Scharff, local rancher Marcus Haines, and I caught and held birds individually for banding. I was shown how to grab from behind and hold each wing next to the body. Otherwise, geese defend or attack with their powerful wings, as I quickly learned. The strong family bonds were amply demonstrated by several ganders that, after release, refused to leave but tried to get over the netting and back to their mate.

Those years of banding at Boca Lake showed a post-breeding movement northward and into Alberta, Canada. One of those bands from our July 1, 1942, drive was returned by a hunter who recovered it twenty-one years later at Crowley, Oregon, about sixty miles northeast of the banding site. By far the largest goose that day was a hybrid Canada/barnyard goose.

The pinnacle of new awakenings and adventures for a sixteen-year-old birder from the Portland Audubon Society came July 8, 1942, while canoeing on the vastness of Malheur Lake. My guide was Ray Erickson, whose graduate thesis was on canvasback breeding habits. Malheur Lake at the southern margin of the breeding range was notable then with three hundred breeding canvasback. Erickson later became Malheur Refuge biologist and went on to the Division of Wildlife Research when the endangered species program was underway. Ray, among other challenges, worked with captive-reared whooping cranes.

Striking out from the south shore just west of Cole Island Ridge Dike, we threaded our way into the heart of the then forty-thousand-acre vastness of ever-fluctuating Malheur Lake. The uproar from mixed calls produced by a host of marsh dwellers grew. For nine hours we paddled or gingerly hopped off onto floating islands and muskrat houses to examine nests.

Ray told me about the dominant hard-stem bulrush (tule), which emerges head high from the deep water marsh to provide cover and attachment, or that forms floating islands for colonial nesters. In winters past when the lake froze hard, the spring ice break-up, accompanied by strong winds, simply mowed down the bulrush and matted, rolled, and wove it into floating masses that would support a person who stepped gently.

Our first nesting colony was of eared grebes. Adapted from my diary:

In most all cases the grebes slipped off their floating nest after covering it. A typical nest I examined had seven chalky white eggs, although when first laid they are a light blue. The eggs were completely covered with dead bulrush of which the nest was also composed. It was a strong structure, well woven and floating freely. The eggs were warm, showing that the grebes left quietly at our approach. One nest had fresh water milfoil for a lining. . . .

We visited a large colony of white pelican who along with Farallon cormorants (double-crested cormorant) were on one of those floating islands. The cormorants were through nesting, and the nearly full grown young took readily to the water but could not yet fly. It was interesting to see them open their bills wide and gulp in air before diving. One nest had two eggs and two newly hatched young that were coal black and naked. When I held them they felt like fat greasy blobs. It seemed like they would melt in the sun.

. . . Ray said the colony was only one-fourth of what it had originally been because winds had broken the island apart. There were abandoned nests and dead nearly grown young, along with eggs lying about, mute testimony to nature's natural control of a species. Ray said about one-eighth of the young birds would reach adulthood. . . . Around the nests were little piles of regurgitated minnows. This tule island must have contained several acres at first, and it was strong enough in places to support me. The nests were all made of this material and built up about a foot off the surface. The water here was seven feet deep.

Treganza's heron (great blue heron subspecies)—of all the young birds I saw, I would give first prize for homely baby to the blue heron. The nest contained three young, originally four as one caught its neck in the woven tule and strangled. At our approach the young herons crawled into the water.... By grasping and pulling with their bills and pushing with feet and wings they moved inch by inch. It was a funny awkward attempt. We caught them and put them back in the nest while they gave low quawks and stabs.

. . . Black-crowned night heron—I saw many young in all stages. The funniest thing was to hear one screeching for its parents when it got into a coot's nesting territory. Every time it was pecked it would squawk. . . . Nests averaged a foot off the tule island surface and one was two and a half feet. They are composed of dead tule and the eggs are blue.

White-faced glossy ibis—this was the best find of the day. While in the Forster's tern colony I asked Ray, rather wishfully, if it would be possible to see one of these birds. "Not very," was his reply. "They are pretty scarce." A few minutes later and Ray exclaimed, "There are your birds, Tom." Was I ever thrilled! We flushed this pair from the tules, about twenty yards ahead of the canoe, and soon after another pair. They flew in wide low circles, black bodies turning an iridescent green and purplish bronze when the sun struck them.

Banding short-eared owls, July 8, 1942. Photo: Ray Erickson.

We immediately began hunting for a nest and soon found it. It was composed of inward bent rushes interwoven into a basket form. It contained two azure blue eggs, which were cold, indicating incubation had not begun and they were still laying. It was interesting to note that the nest contained no dead material, but was entirely of green bent down rushes growing right there. There was likely another nest as the second ibis pair kept circling us.

Redhead—the first nest (pointed out by Ray) had four covered eggs that were submerged when a ruddy duck took possession by laying fifteen eggs on top of the redhead nest.

The second nest, a fine large floating structure of dead tules with an interwoven ramp of dead tule, had seventeen redhead eggs, which gave her possession over the canvasback who built the nest and laid only three eggs. Ray knew the current ownership because white redhead down lined the nest. The canvasback has sooty down. The redhead would raise the canvasback or kick them out.

A raven located this nest for us, as it had just begun to destroy the eggs and flew at our approach. I saw several ravens over the lake and they must do a large amount of nest destruction. I also saw redhead eggs laying in the open or floating in the water. The probable answer is that before the hen has time to construct a nest she lays eggs wherever.

Canvasback—saw only the above nest which the redhead occupied. Ray is studying this species for his master's degree and has so far located twenty-five nests. This is the southern extent of their range with about three hundred here in the summer.

American coot—the most common marsh nesters. Saw nests containing four, six, and seven creamy eggs speckled dark brown or black. Nests were large affairs of floating woven tule. They had ramp ways common to many of the birds with floating nests. Nests were easy to spot among the tules and the young with their fuzzy red heads. I learned that any queer unknown noise in the marsh was due to the coot with its variety of noisy calls.

Long-billed curlew—a pair among the avocets at Cole Island. Must have had young nearby as they circled us all the while giving their rapid whistling cry.

Avocet—to me the most beautiful of shorebirds along with the black-necked stilt. I saw a colony of twenty pairs scattered along the dike. Most of the nests were on grassy islets although twelve were right in the open on the dike. One was right in the car track on top. They were hollow depressions and composed of dried grayish stems of *Atriplex* scattered thinly on the ground.

The eggs, like most other shorebird eggs, were triangular in shape, large at one end and tapered to a point. They were olive green and heavily blotched brown or blackish. The nests had been placed on the road due to high water. Those at the edge of the dike were a platform and contained three, four, six, and seven eggs with an average of four. Where there were seven I believe some pairs shared a nest. One avocet nest with three eggs was built over another with three. Eggs at the water edge were covered with clayish grey mud, probably from adults with dirty feet and breasts. Nests above the water had perfectly clean eggs.

Forster's tern—we visited a large colony. The nests were on another floating tule island, and the eggs lay in a slightly built up depression of dead tule. I saw three to four eggs in a nest. They were drab olive green and heavily blotched dark brown. It was a sight to see hundreds of these dainty white terns hovering overhead against the blue. All were crying in a harsh *keer keer* note. One pair, on [our] approaching their nest power dove and missed our heads by inches. When downwind of these colonies the odor tells you they are there. The worst odor was when Ray broke a rotten pelican egg.

We didn't dare look upward for fear of getting splattered, as the terns were letting go with a lot of whitewash, maybe accidentally on purpose, although I really couldn't say. For neighbors the terns had that colony of eared grebes and also the ibises.

One of the most interesting things seen and explained to me by Ray was the male damselfly carrying his mate who was laying eggs. After mating, the male clasps the female, who would otherwise drown, around the neck with his tail pincers and carries her over the water, while she inserts the eggs through her tail into the pond weeds.

I also learned bulrush stems are quite palatable when the green epidermis is scraped off. It has a sweet juicy flavor, is a little starchy, and a favorite food of the muskrat that I watched eating it. Ray also taught me new terms, *altricial* for birds raised in the nest and *precocial* referring to those like ducklings ready to go on hatching."

In total from my diary we saw seventy-six species that July 8, 1942, including my first Franklin's gull. Other than that host of nesting wildfowl and the muskrats and a few mink this was a day canoeing with a companion and mentor back into time. No sign of man or landmarks. No GPS to get home by—just intuition, the sun's position, bent stem tule markers, and a compass. It was Malheur Marsh at its most productive time.

John Scharff, refuge manager who shaped so many young men in his thirty-six years there, starting with the CCC boys, had taken this young birder from Portland in hand and sent him off with Ray Erickson for the most memorable birding day and summer of his life.

WILLIAM STAFFORD

Malheur before Dawn

An owl sound wandered along the road with me.
I didn't hear it—I breathed it into my ears.

Little ones at first, the stars retired, leaving
polished little circles on the sky for awhile.

Then the sun began to shout from below the horizon.
Throngs of birds campaigned, their music a tent of sound.

From across a pond, out of the mist,
one drake made a V and said its name.

Some vast animal of air began to rouse
from the reeds and lean outward.

Frogs discovered their national anthem again.
I didn't know a ditch could hold so much joy.

So magic a time it was that I was both brave and afraid.
Some day like this might save the world.

Malheur National Wildlife Refuge was formally established in 1908, but John Scharff's remarkable thirty-six-year tenure as manager starting in 1935, when the Blitzen Valley was added to the refuge, in large part making the refuge what we see today. In this oral history, originally presented to the Harney County Bird Festival on April 3, 2005, Dave Marshall and Tom McAllister recount their own time with Scharff. Hendrik Herlyn's transcription of the video is presented in abridged form here—the transcript in its entirety is available from the refuge.

DAVID B. MARSHALL AND TOM MCALLISTER

John Scharff's Malheur

Dave Marshall:
John Scharff served as the Malheur refuge manager from 1935 until his retirement in 1971. He had to retire in 1971 because he was seventy years old and that's the mandatory retirement age for government employees. As [moderator refuge manager Donna Stovall] said, technically he was the second refuge manager. The first one was a man named Stanley G. Jewett, who Tom and I also knew very well. But Jewett never really lived here. Previous to that, the refuge was really managed on a caretaker basis, with people like George M. Benson, who were considered wardens. I remember George Benson real well, too.

John Scharff had the longest tenure of any refuge manager at one station at the time of his retirement, and I imagine that record still holds. I served under him for five years, starting when I was twenty-nine years

old, and as Donna alluded to, he was a great teacher. John Scharff was
born in 1901 in Monument, Oregon, which is in Grant County. His
father was a French immigrant of Basque descent, and his mother was
Scotch. Well, that kind of means the sheep business to me, with those
two ethnic backgrounds, and yes, he grew up with a family sheep business. But his father died at an early age and he had to take over the sheep
business as a boy.

John subsequently went to work for the US Forest Service, starting
as a fire lookout and other jobs and kept working up in the Forest Service. During his early days, he also went to Oregon Agricultural College, Oregon State University today, where he majored in animal hus-
bandry. And then he went back to work for the Forest Service and rose
to assistant supervisor position for the Fremont National Forest, which
is out of Lakeview. Well, John got to be known very well in this part of
the country for his skills in working with grazing problems and with
ranchers, and that meant that the Fish and Wildlife Service wanted him
for Malheur. And they were able to pull him out of the Forest Service
somehow and convince him that he should take over the Malheur Refuge. I want to mention, too, that he married Florence Donaldson, who
came from a ranch near Dayville.

In 1935 he came here to Malheur, and at that time the agency was
called the US Biological Survey instead of the Fish and Wildlife Service.
But his move to Malheur was most fortunate because he had the skills
that were needed to deal with people who were in the livestock business.
He needed to be a local person, he had to have organizational skills. At
the same time, John was a keen observer of wildlife.

In 1935, the Blitzen Valley portion of the refuge was purchased by the
Biological Survey. That created a very hostile anti-government situation.
Local people were not happy, and at that same time, some six hundred
CCC [Civilian Conservation Corps] boys arrived on the scene to help
develop the refuge. When John arrived, there was no control over the
grazing, and the headquarters consisted of a ranch house, the Sodhouse
ranch house, which is gone now, but it was at the present site of the headquarters. Florence and John moved into that ranch house, at which time
the CCC boys began constructing the stone buildings that you see there
now.

The irrigation system, which Peter French started in the Blitzen Valley, was modified and greatly improved by the CCC boys under John's leadership. Another big accomplishment of John's was the numerous private holdings, which were [inholdings] within the refuge—which needed to be purchased or exchanged out. There was no telephone system, and the roads were very primitive. To put it very mildly, it was a rather chaotic situation upon his arrival.

John developed unbelievable compatibility between ranchers and the government. He pioneered haying and grazing for waterfowl management on behalf of not only Malheur, but served as a model for other wildlife refuges as well. The former director of the service, Ira N. Gabrielson, in particular spoke highly of John in that respect. All of the major dams you see on the Blitzen Valley were done when he was in charge. I think one of the biggest accomplishments he was involved with was some sixty transactions involving eliminating the private holdings that were within the refuge and purchasing them or involving other exchanges with BLM or whatever so you didn't have all these private holdings within the refuge.

John's wife Florence, I think, deserves much of the credit. She would never admit to that, but in just my time there, I found that Florence ran what amounted to a guest house for official and unofficial visitors that ranged from local people to US Senators. A core of various naturalists were coming and going, and scientists, and Washington brass, and visiting ranchers. One of the key visitors was William O. Douglas, Justice of the Supreme Court, and he would suddenly appear—John would never say he's coming or anything, but you'd find him there at the house. And that was probably unknown to the press at that time, I don't know [chuckles]. I don't think he would have said anything. Florence was an outstanding hostess and served meals in a very formal manner. She was a very formal person. And as I said, Florence told me that John wouldn't listen to her, but I really think that Florence had a definite role in John's success.

I was told by Ray Erickson, my predecessor, that I couldn't expect that my job description [would be] just the way the position description said. My position description said that I was to be a technical advisor to John on biological matters, but that was not the case. John ran things his own way and you could get things done by showing him, but you could never tell him. He right away let you know that he was running that refuge and no one below him or above him was going to tell him how to run it. So, no one bossed him either from below or on high. You wonder how he accomplished that—well, when you think about it, go back to those visitors at the house, Justice Douglas, senators, congressmen. Even if the regional office or the Washington office wanted to touch John and move him down or move him out or something, they couldn't do it—he was fixed, he was really in place by his influence.

So, as I said, he did what he wanted to do. He would not put anyone in charge when he was away. He was on the national BLM advisory board, which took him to Washington, DC, frequently, and the regional office in Portland would say, "Who's in charge?" and he'd say, "Nobody's in charge. They all know what their jobs are. Nobody needs to be in charge, unless there's a fire." And that was true, there'd be a fire boss if there was a fire, but otherwise, nobody was in charge. And that used to burn the regional office. They didn't know who to call if an issue came up. They wanted somebody in charge, but John wouldn't have it that way.

John had another interesting characteristic. If an employee was thought to be out of line or if [he had] one who tried to dictate to him, or if an employee got to feeling too important, John would take that person out for a day or two of manual work, manual labor, and John would go with that person and work right along with him. And one of the jobs was shoveling manure to make dams during the spring migration that would go in some of the canals and ditches to spread the water, and that was a combination of manure and straw that was often used. So, you'd find yourself working along beside John, putting in little dams.

One day, I criticized John because there were no refuge boundary signs around Mud Lake. I said, "How can that be, you don't have the refuge posted?" Well, I had to spend the next two or three days posting, putting up those signs myself, digging the post holes and so forth. So I learned that I better just keep quiet on those kinds of things.

John also took the law into his own hands. He got along fine with the state enforcement officer, John McKelvey, but he didn't like the federal enforcement agents, and even if they showed up, he'd usually send them away. He'd take care of his own enforcement problems. And just to give you an example of one of the issues, one time he found a group of characters one early Sunday morning sleeping on the refuge in the sagebrush with a fire going during fire season. Well, it turned out these guys were prominent citizens of Burns who were attending the Order of the Antelope activity on Hart Mountain, which was kind of an old boys' drinking party, and they couldn't quite make it back to Burns, and so they decided to spend the night on the refuge beside their fire. Well, John often wandered around the refuge just right after daylight and he found them, and, being John, he took care of that his own way. He told them they had a choice: They could come into town here and see the judge, or they could work it off during the day working for him. He had a lot of odd jobs that needed to be done, manual labor. Well, you know what they chose. They didn't want their name in the paper, so they worked for the day on the refuge.

John and Florence Scharff at Malheur Headquarters "flower wall," 1942. Photo courtesy Malheur NWR.

He did not follow the rules. He wanted to know what the rules were, and the clerk was always reminding him, the administrative officer, where he was doing something wrong, not according to the refuge manual or the Fish and Wildlife Service manual. He said he appreciated knowing what the rules were, but that's not necessarily what he was going to do. Another example of that: When I arrived here on the refuge, soon after I arrived, I'd met everybody and all the staff, and I was driving down Hwy 205 toward Frenchglen, and here was a guy driving a refuge dump truck. And I thought, "He's not one of our staff—who is he? Could he have stolen that dump truck or . . . but no, who would steal a dump truck? No, I don't think anybody could have stolen that." And I thought, "I wonder who that is," and I decided not to do anything until I got back that evening, and I asked John and I said, "There was this stranger driving a dump truck, one of our dump trucks." And John says, "He's no stranger. That's Freddy Witzel." And I said, "But he doesn't have a government driver's license," and John said, "No." And

I said, "How can you do that?" "Well, we use his tractor, so he uses our dump truck." And that seemed kind of strange, but then I began to catch on to these things, that's the way John operated, and then he reminded me that if we didn't have a tractor at the P Ranch and if we were to use a tractor at the P Ranch, we would have to trailer it all the way from headquarters to Frenchglen, and that didn't make sense. It made a lot more sense to use the rancher's tractor. And Freddy Witzel also kept the trash out from behind the dam . . . the bridge on Witzel Lane, he did a lot of service, and I gradually found out that permittees did all kinds of service in terms of irrigation and whatnot.

John counted cattle on and off the refuge personally, and nobody else did it. But any rancher who slipped in some additional cows above his permit—that was it! No more! He was out. And so he was greatly respected.

High officials would often come to the refuge, Washington brass or whatever, to inspect things, and they usually had a list of things they wanted to see that they heard needed to be done, but he would seldom take them to things that needed to be done. He would get them thoroughly confused as to where they were. If it was in the fall, or late summer, he would not take the Center Patrol Road to the Blitzen Valley, but he would go through a series of meadows. And it would be from gate to gate to gate, and they'd see lots of deer, there were lots of deer here then, and so they'd have a real good wildlife show.

One of the things that John loved to do was to put the highest-ranked brass in the right front seat. Well, that meant that guy had to open and close the gates. And you know these gates, these wire gates with the lever that goes around, well, that's kind of an Eastern Oregon thing, and John used to like to watch, look through the rearview mirror on his vehicle and watch this brass open or close one of those gates, and wonder how long it'd take him to figure out how to do it. And he'd sit there and smile and watch on the gate, and if I was there, I'd say, "Oh, I'll go and help the guy close the gate," and he'd say, "Oh, no, no, no, leave him alone . . ." [chuckles]

Well, they never got to see exactly what they wanted to see, but they could hardly criticize things because of what they saw. And one of the things that was an issue was that many homestead cabins were on the refuge, and they got flooded out, most of them did. But the homestead cabins, the old ones that were abandoned, were considered a case where somebody could get hurt in them, and so the brass always wanted to see them destroyed, but John didn't want to do that.

I wanted to mention that early during his tenure as the manager of the Malheur refuge, he was offered the position of regional refuge supervisor in the regional office in Portland. I found this out by going through his personnel folder when I wrote him up for the Distinguished Service Award, the Department of Interior science award. And here was the offer for a promotion in Portland after, this was probably about 1940, a year or just before, to be in charge of all the refuges in the Pacific states. And John's response to this offer to move to Portland was, he couldn't do that because of ill health. So that ended that, he turned it down because of ill health.

John never went by the clock, [he went] by the daylight, he didn't use a watch very much. In fact, he had a pocket watch, but particularly if he was going somewhere, trying to get that pocket watch out of his pocket, you know, when he was sitting down, was almost impossible. So you'd be driving along with him when you went out with him, and it be about . . . get to be starting to get dark about nine o'clock, and you'd be way out somewhere and he'd say, "You know, it must be getting near dinnertime. And I told Florence we'd be in at seven o'clock. But here it's nine o'clock, finding I discover." He just never knew what time it was. He went, he just worked, starting at . . . first thing he did in the morning was milk his cow, and then he'd often go right out on the field before the office ever opened, on the refuge, and look at things. So he'd never come in till dark.

If he needed a favor from a rancher, he would pay them a lengthy visit and discuss the children, and how the cattle were doing, and what the water situation was, and it was just a lengthy visit, and at the last minute, about the time he was ready to leave, he'd bring up what he wanted—that favor of the rancher. I really had a lesson on this when we did the rotenone operation for poisoning the carp in 1955. He took me to meet some of these ranchers and he would talk about all these things that meant nothing to me. And then, about the time we were to leave, he'd say "Say Joe," or whoever it was, "we're going to be conducting a fish poisoning operation and it's going to affect your creek in front of your house and the trout will be poisoned. But we'll replant it right back," which we did, and the rancher or whoever said, "Sure, John, anything you want to do." And then, off we'd go to the next one. That went on till dark, but he had the okay of every rancher in the upstream areas that were involved in this carp control operation.

He refused to lock the office. Can you imagine a government office open all night, that wasn't locked? But the office would not be locked. We had a primitive telephone system with a cranking-type telephone, and there were no telephones on the ranches, and he felt obligated to keep that telephone line open to ranchers and local neighbors in case there was an emergency or whatever. So, local people would come either to his house or the office phone—those were the two phones at headquarters—and use the phone regularly. And then John told me one day, "You know, that's one way you really keep abreast of things, because you can overhear what's going on on the phone."

Following their retirement in 1971, John and Florence purchased a home in Hines. It was that year that John was given the Distinguished Service Award and went back to Washington to receive it with Florence. Florence and John were married for sixty-eight years before Florence's death. John died at age ninety-six in 1988. Florence died a year preceding him.

So that's my story about John, and I would like to say that in his last years, many of you know that John was heavily criticized by some of the extreme environmentalists for his grazing and haying program and water management practices. And I think time is showing that John was very much right in the way he managed the refuge, and it's nice that we have a staff here today that realizes some of the things which have deteriorated at the refuge in terms of wildlife use, and it has. There are just not the birds out there that there were during John's time, for various reasons. Different management practices, different water management practices, because of the carp issue, and I'm very pleased that the present staff is well aware of the challenges which are ahead of them in habitat restoration.

Florence was a great gardener and the headquarters area was quite a showplace at that time. What's the office today was their home, and you can see the row of flowers there, and I'm not advocating that that should be done again, because it's terribly expensive, but it was mostly Florence's volunteer labor that made all that beautiful garden possible. My son used to like to work in that garden; he had figured out how to catch humming-birds in his hand. When one would go in a flower, he would grab at the hummingbird. He became pretty skillful catching hummingbirds.

Tom McAllister [midstream in the interview]:
I had hands-on experience out there with John and his staff, but I also got to know some of the locals. And in particular, the Frenchglen Hotel was not catering to largely tourists and birders, it was the stockmen coming and going through the country and a few of the miners, particularly those who were looking for cinnabar or mercury or in the Pueblos in the south-ern end there at that time. The sheepmen were still running the big bands, and they would leave a car at Frenchglen, and instructions and a map, and Mrs. MacDonald's son Finley and I would drive out to the sheep camp to take them supplies or to pick them up. Sometimes it would be the owner to go out to check on his camp. Well, the first one I went to was the Herlihy [sp.?] camp in the Jackass Mountains, and the Herlihys had a tender out there, his name was Pat Donegan. [I know] you wonder, well, how does he remember all that? I kept a diary that summer, that's how I'm able to pick up for you.

Donegan, when we arrived in the camp, he had the sheepherder's ark with the mules that pulled it, and he had two border collies that came running out to greet us, and he was sitting on that little two-step that goes up into the ark, he was sitting on that, waiting for us. And we came up, gave him his mail and his groceries, and then, in particular, we took out what Herlihy had said, "Be sure and slip this to him." You didn't want your herders to get a supply of liquor, because you wanted them on the job at the bands, but they did have a craving, a few of these herders, they needed it, and we had a pint of whiskey, and that's the first thing we gave to Donegan. And he took that pint of whiskey, and us two kids . . . you know, we're standing there, and Donegan just takes his pint of whiskey, and he tips it up, and without batting an eye he drank half that pint, and then he just took and paused, and he looked at us for a minute and he says to us, he says, "What's a home without a mither, what's a drink without anither" [quoted in a broad Irish accent], and he tops the rest of it off.

Then there was Griffith, Will Griffith, the Welshman, and Billy Berry [sp.?], that's where I first saw Dutch oven cooking, in one of the Berry camps, and I later used that in my family camps and hunting camps. And Walt Riddle, I'll never forget him riding in with his team and buckboard, and he stayed at the Frenchglen Hotel that night, and his family came out the next day, and they had probably one of the only Cadillacs in Harney County. Walt Riddle didn't look like he had a bean in his jean, but there was one of the best-off men in the county, very successful cattleman, and he spent his whole summer up on that wonderful Riddle cabin in the head of the Blitzen country, which, fortunately, has been preserved and is representative of that life and time. He first took out along the waterway there, in the end of the 1880s, and then he finally got patented in 1915. Again, I was just fortunate to meet one of the last of those great characters that arrived early on into the country.

John got to know many of these people, and John had so many facets to him. He was fascinated with this, and he was an absolute sponge to soak up the history of this country. And wherever you were traveling with John, it was an ongoing lesson; not only in the natural history and the people, but the history of the country.

Another one of our chores as boys that summer was to go out and get wood. We had a 33 International truck. The way that you kept the ranch houses warm was with juniper wood, and that takes some splitting and a lot of cutting, and when we'd drive out, one or the other of us would drive the International, and the other would stand behind the cab with a twenty-two, and we would shoot jackrabbits coming and going, and we had lots of jackrabbit ears, we cut the ears off. And in 1942, they had still the five cent bounty per pair of ears on jackrabbits. That was a very big thing in the Depression, you know, five cents was a lot of money, particularly to the ranch kids. And the Bredeen [sp.?] brothers, when that store was a typical isolated ranch country general store, they took the wire hoops that we put the ears on, and old man Bredeen would bring them to the county courthouse and sell them for the five cent bounty, and then he would discount one cent on the ledger at the store, that was his handling charge, and that's what kept us in 22 short ammo. And the kids in that country were probably the best shots in the world, because, instead of shooting a jackrabbit sitting, the big thing was to shoot them on the run.

So these were some of my experiences that summer of 1942. Also, going to the dance at the Narrows, where I thought we would go, you know, just after sundown, but we had dinner after the haying was done, and about eleven o'clock, the picnic hamper was made up for the one-o'clock-in-the-morning picnic dinner, as it were, and we all went to the dance at the Narrows at the schoolhouse, and people came from all around the country, and you went to the dance and you danced all night till the sun came up through the window in the morning, and then you went back to do your chores and . . . it was something you don't forget [chuckles]. And then we would go to Charley Barnes's hot springs, his old bath house just on up the road to the south of Frenchglen, and every once in a while, someone's cattle would get out, like Charley Barnes's cattle seemed to be always getting out, and you'd always be taking time out to herd some-body's cattle back into the pasture. But this was the most memorable of my teenage years, was that summer here in Harney County.

In later years, I came back many times. I'd always figure out an assign-ment here in southeast Oregon, and I'd bring my family, and John and Florence would always welcome us, and we'd stay in the CCC building that's right adjacent to the headquarters, that was there then, and we'd just camp out in that building, and then sleep on the tables, throw our bedrolls out up on those long tables in the building there.

One of the things that was impressive, that I think is so important for the birders, that they don't realize, is that between the ranches and the desire for the shade, the trees that were planted, the locusts and the Lombardy poplar—that's what made that oasis, as the migrants flew over, particularly the warblers, and ever so many of the most interesting bird-ing records in the big red-letter day for the birders that come out from the west side [of Oregon] and hang around the headquarters. All of that group of trees that John Scharff himself established there has provided some of the most [records]. The women in particular [planted] the lilac bushes and those yellow roses, [which produced] interesting birding and the best records in the state.

Billy was the name of John's pet pronghorn buck antelope, and one time, with the several does that he had in there, they had five kids, but that was something for the children, was to go out with John Scharff and feed the antelope and watch him . . . sometimes he'd bottle-feed one of those kids. So that was always an attraction. And there was the goose in the box on the roof of the office. That was a goose that was crippled, and John was always picking up birds or animals that he thought would be of interest, and one of the pictures I have in my old files is of John dancing with the sandhill crane that he raised. And of course, if you get them early enough, they'll imprint and think that they're human. So John had this sandhill crane, and then he had Billy, his antelope, with his little harem of does, and they were right there in the enclosure, which was always an attraction.

He was always meeting with groups, not only at the refuge, that would come up to the cabin he and Florence had on Steens Mountain. One summer, the register up there was a hundred and forty three people at the cabin. And then one of the groups that would always love to come up was from Burns, and Florence was very active in that group, and that was the Sunrise Garden Club, the ladies from Burns, and they came up for their big annual wildflower walk up there, out of the cabin.

John was very instrumental in working with his close friends Russ and Mary Pengelly, who established the beginnings of the Desert Trails Association. And the six sections of the desert trail, which extends all the way down—not all sections are complete, but to Mexico—the six sections in Oregon, and they're designated as national trails. Their daughter, Aubra [sp.?]—I remember one of the stories that came down was, when the first section of the trail was put in, instead of establishing a fixed trail you would follow and would have to maintain, it's more adventurous in this great open country, these wide open spaces, to pick your way out through, and that trail is designated by cairns, or rock monuments. So Aubra was employed that summer, and had a couple of others, and there's some volunteers from the BLM . . . and that's how much of that trail was established, was by designating the route through the cairns. And you could work either way and work your way through the country by following those cairns. And then they had many desert trail trips, where the groups would come, and they would take their backpacks and follow a section of the desert trail. And in the summer, it can get mighty hot, and at the end of one of those big desert trail outings, John Scharff was again the great raconteur historian who would tell the tales at the gatherings, but they'd always remember John coming with the ice-cold watermelons as they came off the end of one of those desert treks—you can imagine how much that appealed to them.

John was working with E. R. Jackman from Oregon State University in a youth program dealing with range management, and they had a youth camp up there in the Logan Valley [near John Day] that John and Florence participated in every summer, working with the youngsters up there in the range camp, teaching good range management. And then there were youth tours, there was a national group came here, and then Beaverton High School was responsible for bringing together some of the best and brightest that would be interested in natural resource issues. And where did they come? Not only from the group out of Portland, but those that were picked nationally, they came here, and John was the one that led those groups.

In his local activity, he was president of the Rotary Club, and he was twenty-five years with the Chamber of Commerce on the board here, and then they were very active in their St. Andrews Episcopal Church, and of course, the Garden Club. But when it came to putting Harney County on the map, and what is here to attract people that want to see a great land, I think one of his coups—and I ran onto this in my notes, and we're going to look it up when I get back, I'm going to check through the BBC and see if we can get a copy—but in 1971, John hosted Barry Payne of Bristol, England, who was a major producer for British Broadcasting Corporation, and they didn't come here just for one quick shoot from that distance. This whole retinue from BBC, a production crew, came out here. And they made three different trips, they came and they did it spring, summer, and fall, and that included a trip, pack-trips down into the Blitzen and the Big Indian, and I remember John telling about his concern of all the packs he'd ever had on one of his horses was to have this tens-of-thousand dollars' worth of equipment for the BBC.

He also regularly hosted Bud Beachwood of KOIN-TV, this was the first major outdoors-type program before your present one on Oregon Public Broadcasting. But Bud Beachwood came over here and did many programs, including a great one on the floods of 1981, '2, '3—that period. He did one special one with John up at the Walt Riddle cabin and another one on the fall color in the Steens, so it'd be interesting to find these, maybe, and sometime show them at a future waterfowl festival.

And then, that Steens Mountain book, undoubtedly the most long-running, most successful of all the large, coffee table–type books, and that is now, through Caxton, the printers in Idaho, in its seventh edition. It first came out in 1967, and it was Charlie Conkling, the photographer from Portland, and E. R. Jackman, and John that did that book. And my favorite writing of John's is the chapter in that book called "The Source of Laughter." John said in there that true humor is a state of mind, and the best place to get that state of mind is out in these big open spaces, like right here in Harney County.

And he starts right out, the first little vignette of humor was about the cowboy who was all bruised and bleeding after he was thrown from his horse, and the cowboy got up and he said, "Well, if the ground hadn't gotten away, I'd still be going yet." Or, "I reached for the saddle horn and I got a handful of dust." And then there was the wonderful one about—this is that dry humor—the sodbuster, and there was a lot of them out here in the Harney Valley and up on the Catlow, the era between about 1900 and 1915–16, and they all went eventually belly-up. It was a dream and it didn't work out, the land wasn't meant for it. And this one, he was so distraught, he went to his neighbor, and he asked to borrow his rifle and one shell. And a week later, he came back and returned it, and his neighbor said, "What was going on with you?" He says, "What were you going to do with it?" And he says, "Well, to tell you the truth, I was going to commit suicide." "Well, why in the hell didn't you?" "Well," the guy says sheepishly, "I just couldn't get nothing but a running shot at myself." And John just loved to tell those stories, he had an infinite number of them.

So here's a man that sprang from the land, was close to the land, but particularly was close to its people. And John—I guess the greatest thing you could say is that he had a faith in man's fairness, everybody he dealt with, he dealt with them on that basis. And when I came over here for his retirement party, Ray Erickson came back to be there with ever so many people, and like Ray said, John showed a basic dignity in his dealings with all people. So this man left his stamp on the land and ever so many of us.

URSULA K. LE GUIN

Harney County Catenaries

Aloof and noble, the great buttes
rear up their rimrock, let
their slopes slide motionlessly down
in the necessary curve from heaven.

What was it like to work at Malheur during the 1950s, when wildlife management was becoming a recognized profession? Young biologists were learning to work alongside the older outdoorsmen—and at that time they were essentially all men—who had built the refuge system from scratch. Dave Marshall, not long returned from service in World War II, shares his own experiences of those transition years in this edited excerpt from his privately published memoir.

DAVID B. MARSHALL

Prize of the 48 States

I once heard Ira N. Gabrielson state he considered "Malheur as the greatest in the National Wildlife Refuge system outside Alaska." I spent time at Malheur as a youngster, and at that point it became a sort of dream that I could someday work there. However, the odds of this happening out of all the positions in the Fish and Wildlife Service seemed slim. But in September of 1955 I left Sacramento behind for an assignment at Malheur that lasted nearly five years. My weekly itinerary report shows we arrived on September 12th after having spent the night in Winnemucca, Nevada. En route we stopped by Fallon [Nevada] to confer with LeRoy Giles.

I did not choose to go to Malheur at the time. Actually I felt I had not finished with all I wanted to do for the Sacramento complex of refuges. However, Ray Erickson, Malheur Refuge biologist, was being transferred to a position in Washington, DC. It is my understanding that John Scharff, who had the longest tenure (thirty-six years) of any refuge man-

The 1937 Mazamas field trip to Malheur. Dave Marshall, age eleven, is thought to be the slight figure with a dark sweater or shirt partly hidden by the front fender of a car just to the right of center. The Scharff home, which doubled as the refuge headquarters, is at right and is still in use today. The three other stone buildings are also still in use by the refuge. Between the left-hand building and the distant trees was where staff housing was located in the 1950s. What remained was destroyed in the high water of the 1980s. Today the complex is encircled by tall trees planted at about the time this photo was taken. Photo courtesy Marshall family, reprinted from Oregon Birds *38(1).*

ager and ran the refuge the Scharff way and not the Fish and Wildlife Service way, depended on Ray to name his replacement. John usually succeeded in dictating who was to be on his staff, much to the chagrin of his immediate supervisor. Ray and I had become close associates because of the Ross's goose study, and I was Ray's choice for his replacement. Thus Ray's move to Washington meant a move to Malheur and a promotion to grade GS-11 for me.

THE SETTING

The Malheur Refuge is located in Harney County in southeastern Oregon south of Burns, the county seat. The refuge is shaped in the form of a lop-sided "T" and covers over 186,000 acres. The largest water bodies in the refuge are Malheur and Harney lakes—that is when they have water. The lakes are in a closed basin (no outlet to the sea) and are fed mainly by the Donner und Blitzen River from the south, the Silvies River from the north, and Silver Creek from the northwest.

The refuge has four major geographical units. The Blitzen Valley extends about forty miles from the south side of Malheur Lake to the west slopes of Steens Mountain. Most of the valley falls within the refuge. Diamond Valley feeds into the Blitzen Valley from the east. The upper portions of Diamond Valley are in private ranches. Most years the waters of Malheur Lake are sufficiently high to flow west through a neck called the Narrows into a smaller lake known as Mud Lake. Mud Lake then drains into Harney Lake, which in many years is little more than an alkaline playa. Adjoining the northwest corner of Harney Lake is the Double O unit of the refuge, which is fed by Silver Creek and springs.

The village of Frenchglen, which has a small hotel, store, school, and residences, is located in the southwest corner of the Blitzen Valley. At least as late as 1939, there was a store at the Narrows, but during my assignment here the Narrows was reduced to two residences. Refuge headquarters is located near the mouth of the Blitzen River at the south side of Malheur Lake.

Adjoining refuge headquarters is a spring-fed pond, known as Sod House Spring, now Marshall Pond. This name came from a sod house built by a homesteader. This was also the site of a Civilian Conservation Corps (CCC) Camp in the mid-1930s. CCC enrollees built, from locally mined stone, five attractive buildings at headquarters as well as two at the Buena Vista station. These buildings have tile roofs, which house numerous bats. During my tenure the stone buildings at headquarters comprised the Refuge Manager's residence, a smaller residence occupied by a maintenance foreman who had a long tenure, a barn, a "service building" that had garage and storage space plus a bachelor apartment, and the office, which also had a bachelor apartment. Subsequently added were an equipment/vehicle repair shop and a museum.

An old ranch house stood under some cottonwood trees located north of the barn. On the east side of the headquarters area was the former CCC Camp, which included a mess hall. During my tenure there, the latter served numerous functions, including a camping site for college classes and a hall for community social functions. The George Benson Museum building was built in about 1954. Also about that time two houses were moved to the north edge of the headquarters area from a government facility near Rome, Malheur County. One of these, adjoining the spring, was assigned to us. Although I replaced Ray Erickson, he was batching at the time and lived in one of the bachelor quarters.

Just east of headquarters was a settlement named Voltage, but it had been abandoned, probably in the 1920s. Five ranches were present within three miles of refuge headquarters along with the Sod House School. The school building, of recent origin then, included an apartment for the teacher and one classroom. Two of the ranches and the school were destroyed by the high water of the late 1980s.

The town of Burns, along with the adjoining town of Hines, are located thirty-two miles north of refuge headquarters. Combined, the two towns had a population of about five thousand people. The entire county, which measures about 75 miles east and west and 150 miles north and south, supports only about seven thousand people today. A high percentage of rural residents possessed an anti-government feeling, in part because the BLM began regulating grazing on public lands starting in the 1930s. Acquisition of the Blitzen Valley by the Fish and Wildlife Service was and remains a factor.

Harney County is basically cattle ranch country, although during our presence, a lumber mill in Hines supplied substantial employment. The ponderosa-pine-covered Blue Mountains lie along the north edge of the county. Steens Mountain rises off the southeast corner of the refuge. Aside from the mountains, the county is largely in sagebrush steppe except for irrigated hay meadows, the refuge, and alkaline playas. Commercial power that came about the time we left made it possible to pump ground water for the growing of alfalfa on several thousand acres east of Burns.

Access to Burns from refuge headquarters was via gravel roads except for the last two miles. During stormy weather, it was not uncommon for the road (State Highway 205) to fill with water of sufficient depth to short out a car's engine in Sunset Valley south of Wright's Point. I also remember getting stuck in the mud on this section of road. The road bed was not elevated, and over time it became a ditch because of dust that blew from it. Thus, it was not practical for permanent year-round refuge employees to live off the refuge.

LIVING ON THE MALHEUR REFUGE

During my assignment, the permanent headquarters staff included the refuge manager, a biologist, an assistant refuge manager, a maintenance foreman, two clerks or administrative assistants, two mechanics, a maintenance man who kept buildings in repair, and another maintenance man who maintained the grounds. Summers saw two to three other employees, including a student assistant who was assigned to the biologist.

Elsewhere in the refuge, there were maintenance positions at three stations, the Double O, Buena Vista, and the P Ranch. Refuge Manager Scharff and his wife Florence occupied the only sizeable and permanent residence at headquarters. The maintenance foreman and his family occupied the only other permanent residence, although the clerk, who had a large family, occupied the old ranch house.

In 1955, our assigned residence at Malheur was an improvement over the made-over CCC barracks at the Sacramento Refuge, but still left a lot to be desired. It had no yard or garage, although eventually this was corrected. Behind the house was a shed that housed a bottled gas-powered generator that provided power for us and two other residences. The shed was also a site for storage of hay, which I fed to our children's horse. The generator, like all others, was subject to breakdowns that made refuge mechanics valuable. Propane provided power for our furnace, refrigerator, cookstove, and lighting.

We lived at this refuge prior to arrival of commercial telephone service to most of Harney County, including the refuge. The CCCs installed a telephone system that ran from Burns south to refuge headquarters, Buena Vista, and Frenchglen. This was a one-line phone with at least six parties on it. At headquarters, phones were present at the office and in the Scharff residence. Obviously the rules were strict in terms of making calls brief, and if you heard voices upon picking up the phone, you were to hang up and wait. The dry-cell-battery–powered phones were of the type you cranked by hand to ring someone. Various combinations of short and long rings were assigned to each location. The line was hooked to commercial service in Burns so one could, if need be, contact parties outside of the system. Maintenance of the lines was a refuge responsibility, and weather, the system's age, and other conditions made searches for breaks in the line a frequent event.

People in today's world are seldom aware of what it was like to live in a sparsely populated community with a manually operated telephone system. For example, one day it became important that I contact John Scharff, who was in Burns on business and running errands, as he typically did. I was spending the day in the office, and cranked the phone to get the Burns operator. I told her I was looking for John Scharff. Her response was, "Where is that John Scharff? I heard he was at the corner by the hardware store talking to (don't remember his name). I'll see what I can do." Word spread and John Scharff called me back within a half hour.

Dave Marshall in his early twenties, prior to his Malheur service, with a young red-winged blackbird.
Photo courtesy Marshall family.

The sparse population also provided other challenges in the way of public services. An example was a visit I made to the Harney County judge[1] with Marcus Haines, a prominent rancher, refuge neighbor, and friend. The visit took place long after my Malheur tenure. We visited the judge to gather information on John Scharff for an award. Upon entering the judge's chambers in the courthouse, we found him asleep at his desk, but he was very cooperative after we woke him up.

Outside the judge's window was a view of the entrance to the county jail. We noted men entering and leaving the jail building. The judge uttered something like this: "Lock them up or let them go free. It is hard to tell what to do. If I close the jail they will do some infraction like urinating on a downtown sidewalk to get back in. If I keep the jail open to them, they are law abiding." It was evident the jail was serving as a homeless shelter and housed no real prisoners.

Some months after that event, the *Oregonian*, Portland's principal newspaper, carried a story on how Harney County was holding people in its jail who were not charged with anything. The tone was extremely critical and charged the county with an illegality. This was a prime example of how city-raised people have little concept of the problems associated with governing an area that lacks facilities they may take for granted.

SOME HARNEY COUNTY CHARACTERS

On my first orientation trip into the Blitzen Valley on September 20th, I met a rancher on a dike coming the opposite way in his pickup. I stopped to visit with him, as is the custom. His first words were, "Who are you?" I introduced myself and said I worked on the refuge. His response was, "You don't work." Later in the day I relayed my experience to John Scharff. He was amused and told me that the rancher, whose name I have forgotten, lived alone at a small ranch on Jack Mountain (originally Jackass Mountain). This placed him about twenty miles from any other individual via unpaved roads.

We were not on the refuge for long before we noticed a man traveling about the area on horseback. Then I noticed the rear end of his horse extending out from a hunter checking station and at other times from abandoned buildings. I was told this was Francis Griffin and that Francis was mentally off. Betty and I picked him up one day when it was apparent he wanted a ride to Burns. This is something Betty did not want to do again because he smelled so bad. Anyway, on the way to town, he explained how he owned Sunset Valley (which he didn't) and all the wild flowers. When we got to town, he said he would purchase us a new Cadillac. I assume one would say he had illusions of grandeur.

We often observed Francis, sometimes camping next to a fire beside the road in very cold weather. I felt sorry for the guy and thought he should be placed in some kind of home. I related this to John Scharff. His response was that Francis was one of the happiest people in the county. In thinking this over, I can see John was right; but at one point he did have to be placed in an institution for reasons of physical health. He told John they were "bathing him to death."

Other than refuge employees, most of the people we had contact with were ranchers and their family members. I found these people were individualists who helped one another. I was called upon to photograph events such as cattle branding, which was done the old-fashioned way by roping the cálves from horses. I also photographed weddings.

WORK ASSIGNMENTS

My assignment as refuge biologist comprised varied activities. The Ross's goose study, initiated while I was stationed at the Sacramento Refuge, continued from the fall of 1955 into the winter of 1956–57 with various trips from Malheur to the Central Valley of California. In addition, I participated in a number of other projects on the Malheur refuge.

CARP POISONING

Upon my arrival, an elaborate operation designed to eliminate carp from the watershed had been devised by the service's fisheries people and was soon underway. The carp, an Old World species, is believed to have been accidentally introduced to the Silvies River watershed in the 1930s with a planting of warm-water game fish. My first trip into the field with John Scharff took place on September 30, 1955, and regarded this project. Several years of low precipitation preceding the carp project had caused Malheur Lake to recede to about ten thousand acres, making the operation feasible. The lake was treated from the air with a contracted surplus World War II, converted Navy Grumman Avenger torpedo bomber starting on or about October 18. The results were spectacular—rows of large dead carp surfaced on Malheur Lake. However, repeated applications failed to kill about two hundred remaining carp that I could readily see from the air in the resulting clear water. Apparently, water conditions had gotten too cold to make the operation fully successful.

In the succeeding several years, sago pondweed again returned to the lake with spectacular results in terms of waterfowl use. A return to good water conditions also helped. For example, just one year after the operation, on a census flight taken October 12, 1956, I estimated there were about 460,000 ducks and geese on the refuge.

Upon the instigation of the carp operation, John instructed me to take photographs of all phases. I was told by the fisheries people this was their job, but John told me to ignore them. Consequently I went ahead, and in the end it was mostly my photos that were used to document and publicize the operation. This was the beginning of extensive photography I conducted on the refuge at John's urging. The photos continue to be used today in various publications.

WILDLIFE INVENTORIES

I found conducting wildlife inventories on this large refuge kept me busy. In fact it was impossible to get a reasonable sample for waterfowl pair counts and brood counts. Included were records on colonial nesting birds. With the student assistant, I also undertook annual surveys of aquatic plant growth on Malheur Lake. Wildlife inventory work on Malheur Lake had to be done by air and air-thrust boat.

One of the most interesting occurrences was the unexpected use of Harney Lake by waterfowl, mainly shovelers. On November 6, 1957, I came up with an estimate of 250,000 of the ducks; collection of several showed them to be exceedingly fat. Further investigations showed the presence of high populations of invertebrates in the lake, including *Daphnia pulex*, *Diaptomus* sp., and copepods, as identified by Dr. Ivan Pratt of Oregon State University. A short drag of a net across the water came up with what looked like hamburger.

Because of the high water that year, a peninsula into the lake became an island. This provided the right environment for two colonial nesting species, white pelicans and Caspian terns. These two species did not otherwise nest on the refuge.

Colonial nesting water birds that nested in large numbers on Malheur Lake included white-faced ibis, snowy and great egrets, black-crowned night herons, great blue herons, and Franklin's gulls. These birds nested in a stand of hardstem bulrush in the center section of the lake, which is now void of such vegetation.

HABITAT MANAGEMENT

Biologically this refuge is complex, but habitat management was largely fixed. Malheur, Mud, and Harney Lakes were and continue to be very much out of refuge control. As described at the beginning of this chapter, they represent the end point of runoff from surrounding mountains. Before these drainages reach the lakes, their waters irrigate thousands of acres of wild hay meadows on both private lands and refuge lands in the Lower Silvies River drainage near Burns, the Blitzen Valley, and Double O area. Water reaching these areas comes primarily in the spring from melting snows in the mountains. Water loss from evaporation occurs mainly in the late summer. Lake levels are, therefore, variable, there being some years when virtually no water reaches the lakes. At other times, there may be several successive years of heavy snowfall, which results in flooding of ranches surrounding Malheur Lake.

Still another complicating factor is water rights. At the time of my tenure on the refuge, those hay meadows with the earliest established rights had first priority when water was in short supply. Refuge lands in the Blitzen Valley were not immune to this. Runoff, of course, occurred in the spring and except where the refuge was able to establish impoundments, hay meadows were drained for haying or naturally dried up.

During my time at Malheur in the early 1950s, numerous ranchers had permits to cut hay in late summer and then turn their livestock into the fields during fall and winter. This policy led to heavy criticism from many in the environmental community who equated grazing in the meadows to damage caused to native upland ecosystems by livestock. Obviously some form of emergent cover is needed, but ducks do not forage or feed in the dense stands of emergent vegetation that occur in the absence of grazing.

In the early 1970s following the tenure of John Scharff, refuge management bowed to public pressure on the livestock issue. The results can be seen today in a decline in bird use. Granted, the irrigation system built by the CCC in the 1930s is partly the problem, since it allows little opportunity to dry a field up to control emergent marsh vegetation such as cattails. My memory of the 1939 Audubon field trip to Malheur remains fixed in my mind. Emergent vegetation was suppressed then due to drought in the early 1930s, resulting in an abundance of birds. In the 1950s, were it not for water rights and the antiquated water distribution system, I would have recommended periodically holding off on irrigation in various meadows to control dense stands of emergent vegetation.

Regarding livestock grazing, I cannot help but remind my environmentalist friends of the spring waterfowl use of hay fields around Burns. Here we have the heaviest spring waterfowl concentrations seen in Oregon—a phenomenon that has led to the annual John Scharff Migratory Bird Festival. Think what the area would look like without haying and grazing—stands of dried emergent vegetation instead of early spring growth for the birds to feed on.

PUBLIC RELATIONS AND EDUCATION

From March into July, there was almost a continuous visitation by biology and wildlife classes from universities in Oregon and Washington, as well as academic professionals and photographers. Some of them were put up in an abandoned ranch house. College classes were put up in the old CCC mess hall. Most visitations occurred on weekends. My weekends were thus filled, and I had almost no time off from April through July. I conducted refuge tours for the university classes, and gave them slide lectures about the area on Saturday nights in the old CCC mess hall. John Scharff spent much time with visitors also. There were no public affairs positions in those days.

Among the visitors were the famous Dr. Arthur Allen of Cornell University and his son. They were present May 11 and 12, 1959, recording bird vocalizations. I spent both days with them, one of which was in the Blue Mountains north of Burns.

My weekly itineraries note that I was a reviewer of the draft of a new western bird field guide sent to me by Roger Tory Peterson in January of 1960. I noted a number of corrections and clarifications that needed to be made.

Annual and twice-annual trips were made to Corvallis to give lectures to classes at Oregon State University. Some of them were combined with student interviews for student assistant positions in collaboration with Gib Bassett, the chief personnel officer from the regional office in Portland. Other lectures were provided to groups like the then Oregon Audubon Society.

As part of the trumpeter swan introduction program discussed below, the pond at headquarters fed by Sod House Spring was surrounded by a fence that held swan cygnets captive when they had been made flightless. I was my job to feed the swans grain every morning. This attracted numerous other waterfowl and also provided a place to hold geese that had been rendered flightless by injuries. We called the pond "the display pool." By placing a blind next to the pond, I was able to photograph numerous waterfowl species, and other photographers took advantage of it as well.

During the spring of 1960, Harold Moulton, on behalf of the Oregon Audubon Society, headed up a project that involved the construction of a permanent photo blind next to the display pool. It was dedicated to William L. Finley and Herman T. Bohlman by the Audubon group. Unfortunately, the floods of the 1980s and resulting moving ice destroyed the blind, despite its sturdy stone construction.[2]

WILDLIFE PHOTOGRAPHY

John Scharff encouraged me to add to the refuge photo collection. Friend and refuge visitor Mike Wotten and I built a photo blind on stilts, which was placed in an egret colony. This afforded the opportunity to photograph the birds at close range. However, the following winter the blind was knocked down by moving ice. I also photographed sandhill cranes. One of my photos of two dancing cranes was widely used in Burns. A mural in a grocery store that stood for several years was modeled from it, and the crane pair forms a logo used for the annual John Scharff Migratory Bird Festival.

CONDUCTING AN ORNITHOLOGY COURSE

During the course of my tenure at Malheur, Eleanor Pruitt and her then husband, Ken, co-managers of the Frenchglen Hotel, were frequent cooperators. In this regard, I followed Ray Erickson's footsteps by ending Saturday field trips for college classes with dinner at the hotel. Eleanor liked to accommodate such groups and put together dinners that were moderately priced for the students. She was interested in wildlife and at times accompanied me to observe sights like heron colonies in Malheur Lake. Near the end of my Malheur assignment, she took it upon herself to set up a situation whereby I would teach a course in ornithology through the Oregon State Extension Service. Surprisingly, seventeen people signed up, including local teachers who were looking for such subjects to maintain their teaching credentials. I gave the lectures at night in Burns and on Saturdays took the class on field trips. The course provided the students three college credits. This was my first real teaching experience. I enjoyed it and acquired some new friends.

THE GEORGE M. BENSON MEMORIAL MUSEUM

The natural history museum that now stands at Malheur headquarters goes back to George M. Benson, who, as near as I can tell, was the refuge's first full-time employee. I do not know when Benson gained employment by the refuge, but he was active during the 1930s and resided on the refuge. Prior to Benson's tenure, several individuals had held the position of warden for the refuge beginning with its establishment, including Dr. E. L. Hibbard and George Cantwell.

I first met Benson during the week spent at Malheur with Stanley G. Jewett and the Oregon Audubon Society in 1939. He spent several days with us and directed us to various sites with his government-issue Ford V-8 pickup, which was about 1936 vintage. At that time Benson and his wife lived on the east edge of what we know today as Benson Pond, which is located on the southeast side of the Blitzen Valley. The house has long since been razed. The Audubon group visited the residence, which I remember well for all the mounted bird specimens that decorated the house's interior. Benson had taken a mail-order course in taxidermy, which was advertised in sporting magazines. On a high kitchen shelf was a lineup of mounted owls, but one of them was obviously not mounted. Its eyes blinked; it turned out to be a pet flammulated owl.

Ray Erickson told me that after Benson died, the specimens remained at refuge headquarters in storage. Finally, in desperation, Ray placed a statement in his weekly activity report that he was boxing up the specimens for shipment to the US National Museum. J. Clark Salyer picked up on this and announced, "I will provide the money for a museum." The museum was completed shortly before my arrival at Malheur.

Ray, probably with assistance from Pat Hansen, had placed Benson's mounted birds in display cases; however, a number of prominent species were missing. I helped fill this void with some collecting. Pat Hansen did the mounting. She is a real artist who did some fine wildlife drawings and resides today in Santa Rosa, California. Pat came to Malheur in about 1954 with her husband, Charles, who was an OSU graduate student at the time. One of my duties was to periodically fumigate the specimens and otherwise care for the museum. I suspect the plant specimens Ray and I collected remain housed there, too. The George M. Benson Museum remains as an important education facility at Malheur today.

I must add that George Benson was an active bird bander who had a waterfowl banding trap along the Blitzen River below headquarters. It is my understanding that he was originally a homesteader near refuge headquarters. During my tenure at the refuge, we received a notice from the General Services Administration that old files should be destroyed in order to save space. The clerk of the time took this seriously and began the process of destroying Benson's files, which were located in the refuge basement. I was able to stop him before he could finish this task.

Among the files rescued were precious memos Benson had written to the regional office. One related to a dispute over his qualifying for mileage for an official trip to Bend, for which he took his personally owned Chevrolet instead of the government Model T Ford Roadster pickup. It was during a cold spell, and he wrote that anyone knows you don't start a Model T in 20 below temperatures. I discovered times had not changed. Elsewhere there was a list of repairs undertaken on the Model T by the Burns Garage. It included an engine valve at a cost of three cents. I wonder what happened to those files, which would now be of great historical value.

HUNTING PROGRAMS

The first year of my assignment, or the previous year, saw the establishment of a public hunting area for waterfowl at the west end of Malheur Lake. The program was run in part by the state, but it was our job to post the area and provide other assistance. I played a role in this by assisting state personnel in checking hunters in and out of the area, preparing maps for handouts, etc. I do not feel the operation was a complete success for lack of hunter access. Even with boats, they barely penetrated the area open to them, and it was common to have to pull hunter vehicles from mud holes in the access road once the rains came.

My close friend Tom McAllister was the outdoor editor for the *Oregon Journal* at the time. I took him and a friend out on the lake for a successful canvasback hunt on October 14, 1957. Hunting never really excited me. My lack of skill showed up on this hunt when I accidentally pulled both triggers of my grandfather's 10-gauge double-barreled shotgun and was thrown backwards onto the ground. Our Labrador retriever, Katy, who was so skilled in retrieving sick and crippled ducks, refused to collect dead ones, as she had been taught with botulism victims.

TRUMPETER SWAN PROGRAM

Malheur had long been considered a potential site for establishing a breeding population of trumpeter swans. The main population of this species, as known at that time, was at the Red Rock Lakes Refuge in Montana. The intent behind the transplant was to establish a population outside the Red Rock Lakes area should some disaster hit them there. A transplant was attempted starting in the 1940s with pinioned birds held at the Double O in a large enclosure. This transplant was unsuccessful due mainly to the fact that nesting trumpeters are highly territorial and their territories are large.

In the mid-1950s, we tried another approach, specifically to capture immature and cygnet trumpeters at Red Rock, take them to Malheur, clip one wing so they would remain flightless until the following year, and place them in the display pool mentioned above.

Members of the Red Rock Lakes Refuge staff delivered seventeen swans to us on September 28, 1955, and eleven more on August 11, 1956. On September 25, 1957, I drove to Red Rock Lakes Refuge and picked up another twenty swan cygnets. I arrived back at Malheur the following day. I transported them in a half-ton Dodge pickup that had a poultry wire enclosure over the bed. Burlap covered the top of the enclosure. On this trip, I recall helping capture seven of these birds from an airboat, but thirteen had already been captured and placed headfirst in burlap sacks with a hole cut through the bottom of the sack from which the head and neck could extend. While this restrained the birds, I felt it was not right for those birds to be left immobile on the Red Rocks Refuge shop floor, and made the decision to drive back to Malheur without waiting for a night's rest. I had the birds removed from the sacks before placing them in the pickup. I made frequent stops to wet down the burlap top so water could drip on the birds and keep them cool. That was the longest period I ever went without rest. I don't think this would have been approved of today from a safety standpoint.

One comical event occurred on this trip. I stopped at a restaurant in a small Idaho town. The pickup with a US Fish and Wildlife Service logo on the door and a load of swans, of course, attracted attention. Diners next to the window saw me exit from the pickup and come in to eat. The restaurant owner was spouting off on how he had just been cited for a game law violation. He said, in reference to the wildlife people, "The next one of those guys who comes in—I will poison him, by God." The restaurant patrons roared with laughter. Little did he know that to a small town, I was one of "those guys."

The swans did fine in the pool at headquarters, although a bobcat got in and killed several. They eventually became free flyers, but regularly came into the pond to feed on grain that was placed in the water each morning. On March 5, 1958, I accounted for a minimum of twenty-eight trumpeters as being present on the refuge. Then, on a flight over Malheur Lake on August 6th, Ray Glahn and I looked down on a brood of two trumpeter swan cygnets. This was the first success from many years of effort. It turned out there were actually two broods of two birds each that hatched that year. In September of 1958, student trainee Dale Hein brought in four more of the birds from Red Rock Lakes. Trumpeters have continued to breed at Malheur, although in numbers fewer than ten.

PROPOSED DAM ON SILVIES RIVER

During my tenure at Malheur, a proposal emerged to place a dam on the Silvies River and convert the privately owned meadows in the Lower Silvies River floodplain from flood type irrigation systems to leveled fields using sprinklers. The Fish and Wildlife Service Division of River Basin Studies (now Ecological Services) asked me to evaluate the proposal, particularly with respect to the spring waterfowl migration on the floodplain. I conducted several waterfowl inventories that documented the importance of the floodplain. The proposal was eventually dropped. However, this provided an opportunity for the first time to document the heavy spring waterfowl use of the Lower Silvies River floodplain, otherwise called Harney Valley. For example, on an aerial census conducted in the spring of 1958, I estimated the presence of seventy-three thousand ducks, twenty-five hundred tundra swans, and forty-five thousand snow geese in the valley.

MISCELLANEOUS ACTIVITIES

Relatively minor outbreaks of avian botulism occurred on Malheur Lake in 1957 and succeeding years. One of my jobs was to retrieve sick ducks and hospitalize them. I also had assignments and quotas for waterfowl banding. I was not nearly as successful at trapping ducks as my replacement, Gene Kridler, but nonetheless did band hundreds, including migrants and ducklings produced locally. Another assignment involved dividing up muskrat hides with trappers. The government got a share of these.

At least two wildfires occurred during my time at Malheur. A lightning fire took place near Vickers Lake, which is a part of the west end of Malheur Lake. Due to its isolation, I served as an aerial observer tracking control activities and its progress. The other fire spread from an exploding stove at the Buena Vista Station east into Diamond Valley in a matter of a few hours. I was on the fire line all night. I think this was the only time I received overtime with the service.

About the dumbest program I ever got involved with was the capture of about a thousand California quail, which were held at refuge headquarters and transferred to the Portland International Airport for air shipment to the Virgin Islands. As explained to me, the Virgin Islands ambassador was a California quail fan and was sure they would survive there. Through the State Department and politicians in Washington, he saw to it that the service provided the quail. Obviously, they did not survive.

There were several instances when I observed birds at Malheur that constituted new distributional records for their species. I followed up by collecting the birds, usually with my .410 shotgun and dust shot. This was the only acceptable procedure for establishing new records, at least until the 1970s, without telephoto-lens cameras or confirmation by other qualified people. A bird was collected, made into a study skin, and sent to a reputable museum, at which point editors of ornithological journals would accept such records for publication.

For example, I established the first state records for the Phainopepla on May 18, 1957, and the black-throated blue warbler on October 9, 1957, by collecting and sending them to the US National Museum in Washington, DC. Gene Kridler, who held my Malheur position in later years, was one of the top banders and collectors of vagrant bird records using mist nets. Gene and I wrote and published a joint paper on various bird records from Malheur.

Time had to be spent writing the quarterly refuge narrative reports, which provided a summary of events, activities, and wildlife observations for the periods involved. I regret these reports are no longer written for refuges, as they present a historical record over time.

TRANSFER TO THE REGIONAL OFFICE

When they established a regional refuge biologist position in Portland, I was selected after a short period in which Watson Beed served. My official departure from Malheur was on August 13, 1960.

MALHEUR REVISITED

Visiting Malheur today is rather emotional for me. I see the decline in bird use of the Blitzen Valley, but most of all I see that Malheur Lake is nowhere near what it was during the late 1950s. Carp were nearly eliminated from the lake in 1955 when waters were low and only the central, lowest part of the lake, was inundated. The following years saw water levels return to normal and sago pondweed returned. The lake center, particularly, had an ideal interspersion of hardstem bulrush patches with open water. The birds responded with great nesting colonies of terns, herons, ibis, and egrets. Waterfowl visitation during the spring and fall migrations included thousands of tundra swans and canvasbacks, which fed on the sago pondweed.

In succeeding years carp numbers climbed again, resulting in the loss of sago pondweed. Then came the floods of the 1980s, which completely inundated and killed the hardstem bulrush patches in the center unit of the lake. This area stands today as open water with no cover except along the lake edges. The floods also destroyed Cole Island Dike, which had been washed out at one point years ago, but served as an access point to the lake for birding.

Malheur Lake will not be what it once was until the central habitat area is restored. This is the heart of the refuge, a fact that seems to go unknown to the public for lack of access. I will leave the solutions to another time, but they would be costly in terms of dollars. Some advocates have pushed to have Malheur Lake designated as wilderness area, but to me it does not qualify. It is not a naturally functioning ecosystem due to carp infestations and upstream water diversions.

Dave Marshall at Malheur centennial in 2008.
Photo courtesy Marshall family.

Despite the sad condition of the Malheur Refuge today, I see some positive aspects. Progress has been made in controlling carp in some Blitzen Valley ponds by screening water control structures. A large structure has been built between Malheur and Mud Lakes that screens out adult carp.

Merchants in the town of Burns recognize the economic gains brought by visiting birders, and of course the number of birders has grown many times over since the 1950s. And finally, the tree plantings made by John and Florence Scharff serve as an oasis or attractant for migrating songbirds. Birders gather here in the spring to make unusual records of vagrant warblers and other out-of-normal range species.

Notes

1   In some rural Oregon counties, the term "county judge" means the chair of the board of county commissioners. This is still true today and includes Harney County. However, Marshall appears to be referring to what was then called a District Judge and today is known as a Circuit Judge, a traditional judicial officer.
2   Upon Dave Marshall's death in 2011, his widow Georgia Leupold Marshall donated a solid new stone birding blind on the east side of the pond, which was renamed Marshall Pond in honor of Dave's work not only at Malheur, but in the establishment of several other refuges and as senior author of *Birds of Oregon* (OSU Press, 2003).

The next generation of visitors and observers started with Dave's son John Marshall as much as with anyone—he spent part of his childhood on the refuge, doing what children do but also absorbing the air and water of Malheur. Once we absorb this mix, it is always there. John Marshall shares with us some of his memories of being a Malheur child.

JOHN F. MARSHALL

Malheur Childhood

Beneath the ice covering the ditch, I could see the carp moving. Carp were both fascinating and something bad. I was seven years old and walking home from Sodhouse School. Home was a tiny house at Malheur National Wildlife Refuge headquarters. It was 1958, Dwight Eisenhower was president, and our family was living in one of the remotest places in the United States. I did what I had done before, I picked up a chunk of lava rock and threw it as hard as I could, breaking the ice but leaving the carp unscathed. Malheur was all about protection of wild creatures and celebrating nature, but somehow carp were not included. It was a bit puzzling to me, as I had watched coyotes eat dead carp and had seen a pelican regurgitate a large carp in order to take off on the water.

My father was David B. Marshall, the refuge biologist, and he explained how carp were foreign to Malheur and were destroying the aquatic plants that ducks and geese fed on. The carp problem was so bad that a massive eradication program was implemented where liquid rotenone was poured into all of the waters of the Blitzen Valley and the refuge in order to kill the carp. The dying carp could be herded to shore. For a child it could not be more exciting! Our house was next to the spring-fed display pond, which had trout as well as carp. My sister and I gathered up the trout, which were deemed safe to eat.

Other excitement as a kid living at Malheur included riding in either the airboat or the airplane. The airboat was a flat-bottom aluminum boat with an airplane propeller behind a wire cage. The airboat was the pre-ferred craft for Malheur Lake as it could get around no matter how shal-low. The noise was deafening, so we put cotton in our ears, as hearing protection muffs had not yet been invented. The airboat had no keel and drifted sideways around corners as we meandered by islands of floating bulrushes past the nests of egrets and grebes out on Malheur Lake. A canoe paddle was kept in the airboat in case the motor should fail. There was no radio and it was long before cell phones, so I wonder how that would have worked out.

Ray Glahn, a World War II fighter pilot, was the US Fish and Wild-life Service pilot. He would come several times a year for aerial surveys. Ray was a highly competent pilot and great with kids. My sister Janet and I took turns riding in the tail section of the plane, a Piper Super-Cub, known for being able to fly low and slow. We would know ahead of time when Ray was coming and would ride our bicycles down at the airstrip to watch the plane come in. In the evening, my mother, Betty, would prepare a nice dinner for Ray, as she did for many refuge visitors.

Malheur may seem remote today, but it was far more isolated in the late 1950s. There was no television reception and only one radio station, which played "cowboy music" much to my father's disgust. We did not travel to Burns more often than once a week, as the cost of gas was an issue, and most of the thirty-two miles were gravel. The road was icy in winter, muddy in spring, and dusty the rest of the year. Cars did not have air conditioning, and dust billowed. Opening the windows on hot days was not an option. One day we picked up Francis Griffin, a deranged hobo with a fertile imagination who lived in an abandoned shack near the narrows with his burro, but we didn't realize that he hadn't bathed for a while. Francis spent many a night in jail, not because he had committed a crime, but because the jail doubled as the homeless shelter, and Francis could leave whenever he wanted to.

There was a handful of kids living at refuge headquarters, none of whom my parents thought of as suitable playmates as there were some troubling behaviors. My sister Janet was wrapped up in her horse Lightning and was a very competent bareback rider. I was less athletic and got peeled off the back of the horse when Janet reined the horse under the clothesline, with me sitting behind her. I found other ways to amuse myself. I built roads in the dirt with my road-grader and ran trucks over them. I made wooden boats and bows and arrows out of willow sticks.

I took an interest in insects, particularly butterflies, which I collected. I was outfitted with a net my mother made, and a kill jar, which in keeping with the time had a foam rubber pad soaked with either cyanide or carbon tetrachloride. I pinned the dead insects to a mounting board and later transferred them to a cigar box. Florence Scharff's flower gardens were the best place to capture butterflies. Monarchs and tiger swallowtails were my favorites. One day, I caught a hummingbird with my bare hands by sneaking up on it while it had its head buried in a petunia. I was disappointed that my father did not have a band small enough for a hummingbird! I had one very odd hobby, and that was digging holes in the ground. I wanted to know what was down there. More than once I dug up a spade-foot toad, which appeared to be dead until it ever so slowly flexed a limb.

Arrowhead collecting was not only permitted, it was encouraged. When I was about seven years old I got a bicycle, which allowed me to venture out to look for arrowheads. One day I found myself in a tree two miles from home in Johnny and Georgia Crow's yard with a herd of cattle milling below. The Crows were not home and I was petrified. In retrospect, the cows were just curious, but I had heard all of the warnings about bulls and thought they were out to trample me.

Rattlesnakes were high on my parent's fears as I was out a lot wandering through the sagebrush. I had watched someone milk venom from the fangs of a rattlesnake and feared them too. I never did have a close encounter, but our dog Katy came home with two spots of blood on her nose, and her neck was rapidly swelling. My father immediately figured out what had happened, and used bolt cutters to get her choke collar off before she strangled. Katy lived through the experience without being treated by a veterinarian.

Katy—a huge black Labrador retriever—was my hero, powerful, smart, and playful. Katy was instrumental in the waterfowl banding my father did. In the late summer when ducks molt their feathers, they are temporarily flightless. Dad would set up wing traps at the end of refuge ponds, and Katy would splash through the shallow water driving the ducks as if they were sheep. She could also run down ducks when they were flightless, catch them, and deliver them un-harmed to my father for banding. Dad would see some ducks in a ditch, let Katy out, and she would capture the ducks and bring them to him. Katy did not like coots, as they have claws and would dig into her face. Katy had a sense of humor and loved to run at people, letting them think they were about to be knocked down, missing them by a whisker. She also had a game going with a magpie that came every day to tease the dog. Katy would lunge to catch the bird, which would always be just out of reach. Both dog and magpie seemed to enjoy the game. Being a retriever, Dad decided to try out Katy on waterfowl hunting. Katy had a keen nose, and before Dad could fire a shot, the dog had found a limit of crippled birds hiding in the tules. Between the crippled birds, and being knocked over for having made the mistake of pulling both triggers at the same time on a 10-gauge double-barreled shotgun, Dad had enough of hunting. Sadly, we lost Katy to distemper when she was four years old.

Wildlife encounters were not limited to what could be seen through binoculars. Jim Yocum was a BLM wildlife biologist from Nevada who frequently visited the refuge. Yocum had a pet bobcat named Rufus. I have a memory of Rufus fishing bacon out of a frying pan in our kitchen, as breakfast was being cooked. Unfortunately, Rufus got sick and died. Rufus' replacement was of different temperament and promptly bit me on the wrist when I reached into the back of Jim Yocum's pickup to pet him. John and Florence Scharff had Ellie and Billie—pronghorn antelope—and Eddie the deer in an enclosure on the hillside below where the observation tower is today. These animals had been bottle fed and were very friendly. They were allowed outside of their fenced area and would wander about headquarters. An unfortunate event involving herbicides most likely resulted in these animals becoming sick and dying. The chemical 2,4-D was sprayed on willows that were taking over the display pond. The individual who did the spraying was a brash man who decided that if a little of the chemical was good, a whole lot would be better, and did not follow the label. Sagebrush up on the hill, well away from the pond, died and so did the pet pronghorn and deer.

Although there was something different about being a government family instead of a ranch family, there was a lot of positive interaction and no outright hostility. We attended the rodeo in Crane, cattle drives, and brandings. As a young boy watching brandings and castration of calves was traumatic. I can still see Rocky Mountain oysters being plucked out of a steaming pot with tongs. Refuge headquarters was a social center, not just for refuge personnel and birdwatchers, but the ranching community as well. There were potlucks held at the old CCC barracks. I have a memory of a potluck event, where every woman had made a dessert. A curtain was drawn, so that only the ladies' feet could be seen. The men had to pick out which pair of feet corresponded to their favorite dessert. It was the fifties!

The Haines family, who lived just to the west of refuge headquarters, were among our best friends. Marcus Haines was a rancher who ran cattle on the desert near Harney Lake. Teenage daughters Nancy and Susan had two steers that they had raised as a 4-H project and could not give up for auction and slaughter. The steers became pets and could be ridden.

John Scharff and Malheur National Wildlife Refuge were inseparable. Scharff was refuge manager for decades, having started with the Forest Service in its earliest days. John Scharff had only a high school education, but a very sharp mind, and was knowledgeable in many areas. He was particularly good at dealing with people, and was very kind toward me. Scharff was soft-spoken and went about the job at a slow pace, but was never really off duty. The refuge was his life. White-haired Florence Scharff was a very proper lady who devoted her time to making the headquarters grounds beautiful with flower gardens. In the 1970s Malheur came under a lot of criticism for the extent of cattle grazing that had been accommodated by John Scharff. To be sure there were some conflicts between ranching and wildlife. Hay cutting no doubt caused problems for nesting birds and fawning deer. However, grazing and haying had a very important function, and that was to keep the wetlands open. Without grazing or burning, a marsh becomes crowded with vegetation and open water disappears, limiting feeding opportunities for waterfowl. Flooded hayfields become rich feeding grounds. I have memories of cow pies sub-merged in brownish water swarming with invertebrate life.

Steens Mountain was central to the Malheur experience. We loved to camp beneath the aspen trees up on "The Steens," where we could watch bluebirds and flickers enter nest holes. Wildflowers were abundant and the scent of mountain big sagebrush hung in the air. Typically, we camped by a small brook. I had a water fascination and would pick the leaves of false hellebore, load them with tiny pebbles, and launch them into the current, pretending they were boats. My first fishing experience was catching trout out of Grove Creek using a willow stick with a leader tied to the end of it and a worm. As a teenager I would return as a fly-fish-erman. Before the Steens Mountain loop road was built, the road up to the top of the Steens was full of large rocks and holes. I remember a car with oil leaking out after hitting a rock, and chewing gum in hopes of plugging the hole. We saw the bad road as a positive in that it limited the number of people who would go up on the Steens. If you did happen to run into someone up there, chances are you knew them or knew of them. Of course any trip to the Steens went by the Frenchglen store, where I would be permitted a Nesbitt's orange soda or an ice cream sandwich. It was also a chance to ogle the fishing tackle on display.

As it is today, Malheur and Steens Mountain was a destination for organized tours. Oregon Audubon Society made a trip once per year, and there were numerous college field trips. My sister Janet and I were placed in separate cars on college field trips ostensibly to identify birds for the college kids. I am not sure to what degree the students did not know the birds, and only pretended not to know them for our benefit. Audubon trips were an all-day affair with too many stops and too much standing around for a young kid. I preferred throwing rocks in the pond to looking through a spotting scope, which did not please my father. Bird watchers were seen as an oddity to the locals. Even among the refuge personnel there was an emphasis on ducks and geese over species that were not hunted. My Dad was belittled as a "dickey bird watcher," something that would probably not happen today. Typically, Audubon field trips ended in Frenchglen, with dinner at the hotel cooked by Eleanor Pruitt. For the city folks, the buckaroos who hung out at Frenchglen in the evenings were a special addition to the Malheur experience. These guys were the real thing, with their hats, chaps and spurs.

There are many more memories that I could talk about, the calling of sandhill cranes, early morning trips to sage grouse dancing grounds, a raccoon working its way paw over paw to reach a dead duck caught in a fence, the frenzied activity of swallows swarming around mud nests on stone buildings, beavers swimming in the central canal, and the hollow jug sound of bitterns. Malheur is a rich place. May it always be a place for wildlife and people who appreciate nature.

PART 3

Desert Pilgrimage

Central to the Malheur experience is water, and central to the basin's water are the Silvies and Donner und Blitzen Rivers. Steens Mountain has been described as "mother of waters and father of storms," and without these waters we would be enjoying a simple steppe desert. With them we have not only birds and the animals who drink from the rivers and their tributaries, but we have denizens of the water itself. We have, among other things, the redband trout. Maitreya has caught them. Sometimes.

MAITREYA

The Soul of the River: Redband Trout

In many ways the story of Malheur National Wildlife Refuge is also the story of the Donner und Blitzen River. In the portion of the refuge that encompasses the Blitzen Valley, those lands from Frenchglen to refuge headquarters, it is the Blitzen River watershed that provides most of the life-sustaining water to the mosaic of fields, marshes, and ponds. Here the Blitzen carries the lifeblood of the refuge; it is the essential circulatory system of the refuge macroorganism. Powering this circulatory system is mighty Steens Mountain, with its hundreds of square miles of surface area capturing vast amounts of rainfall and snowmelt, and its ninety-seven hundred feet of elevation delivering the gravity-driven heartbeat to keep the water moving. And if the Blitzen River is the heart of the refuge, then it is the salmonid fish of the river, the redband trout, that are the soul of the river.

Of course this is a fisherfolk view of the world, this natural human association between a river and the fish that inhabit it. Like the young boys from many human cultures of all generations and all around the world, I grew up a fisherman. For all of the years of my childhood and adolescence, going fishing was a regular family activity. When I reach into the vault of my childhood memories, it is a fishing trip that stands at the beginning: I am three years old in a small boat with my father and two other adults on Renner's Pond southwest of Lakeview, and we are catching trout. About all of the trout that we caught there are countless stories to tell of the rivers, creeks, and lakes that we fished, of battling the elements, or the mosquitoes, or the rattlesnakes in pursuit of those treasured salmonids, of the great pleasure of frying up fresh trout for dinner the same day that we caught them. But the best fish stories are about the ones that got away, those special fish that have the will and the strength and the guile to escape the best efforts of the angler. One of those fish was a Blitzen redband trout.

It was the first week of October 1972, and our family had parked our Terry travel trailer and pitched a tent at Page Springs Campground. While my mother, Donna, remained in camp, my father (Bill), my brother (Russell), and I set out south from the campground, fishing for trout and working our way upstream along the renowned Donner und Blitzen River. It was a gorgeous fall day, a time of the year when water flow in the river is low, making it relatively easy to ford the river as needed, and as we rounded the first bend in the river, we followed the tracks of those who had gone before us and crossed over to the west bank—better that than to bushwhack the rocks and brush on the east side of the canyon.

My tackle that day was an eight-foot, light-duty fly rod set up with a manual fly-fishing reel wound with floating fly line and ten-pound test leader. In my pocket-sized tackle box was an assortment of dozens of dry flies and nymphs, as well as several sizes and colors of Rooster Tail spinning lures. On that day the fish were biting the Rooster Tails and we caught many trout in the eight to twelve inch range, releasing most and saving some for dinner.

A mile upstream from Page Springs Campground there is a concrete weir across the river, approximately four feet tall, that is part of a water-flow gauging station. This weir creates a large slack water pool on the upstream side, and as that upstream pool empties through its central gate, it creates a very powerful rapid, the force of which has carved a large torrent pool on the downstream side of the weir. When we arrived at the weir, Bill and Russell both decided to fish the downstream end of the rapid in the torrent carved pool, wading out into the water about fifty feet downstream of the weir. I, on the other hand, stood on the concrete of the structure itself, right next to the powerful water rushing over the weir. At the previous hole, I had snagged my lure, the one that was working, the white one with silver and gray tones, on a rock and lost it. "Bummer!" Looking in my assortment of flies and lures, I decided to tie on the only Rooster Tail with the same colors as the one I had just lost. Problem was that it was a quarter-ounce size, nearly four inches in length from the tie-on to the end of the tail, not exactly the right choice for the situation and size of trout that we had been catching that day.

Rather than attempting a traditional fly-casting technique with such a heavy lure, I pulled out about twenty feet of line at my feet and dropped the Rooster Tail right next to the weir, under the rapid, and let the force of the current take the line out. This presentation may well have given the impression of an injured fish being carried downstream over the weir, then as the line pulled tight, the Rooster Tail kicked in with its spinning action. Instinctively, I used the tip of the fly rod to work the lure back under the rapid, back toward the weir, and in a flash, fish on! Once hooked, the fish swam downstream with the force of the rapid, quickly taking out fifty feet of line. "Tighten the drag, keep the pole tip high, left hand on the reel, start reeling him in." If not for the fish's next move, there would be no story to tell. The biggest Blitzen redband trout any of us had ever seen jumped completely out of the water, shaking its head from side to side in an effort to drop the lure.

They say that time slows down at moments like this; perhaps it is rather that the shutter speed of memory formation in our brain dramatically increases. For me the image frozen in time is that of the giant redband suspended in midair ten feet in front of my father; for my father it was the image of the giant redband suspended in midair ten feet in front of his face. Over the years, this fishing adventure became one of my father's most repeated stories. In Bill's version of the story, the fish was described as a torpedo, at least thirty inches long and more than five pounds in weight. Still on the hook a few seconds later, the big fish decided to make a second jump, this time slightly downstream, closer to my brother, again all the way out of the water and shaking its head from side to side. After the second jump, the fish changed tactics, positioning itself centrally in the weir outflow rapid, adding the force of the water to its own strength, negating any attempt to reel it in further. Stalemate for a minute or two, then—SNAP!—the ten-pound leader was blown, and the fish was gone.

That Big Fish that got away was part of the population of Malheur Lakes Basin redband trout, which evidence suggests has been isolated from Columbia Basin rainbow trout populations for approximately eighteen thousand years, since the Voltage lava flows blocked Malheur Gap between the present-day Malheur Lake and Malheur River. For many thousands of years, the Blitzen redband trout benefited from a system of reproductive connectivity with redband trout in the Silvies River and Silver Creek. The potential for inter-stream breeding diversity appears to have been lost primarily due to the explosion of carp in Malheur Lake.

Historical records indicate that carp were found in Malheur Lake beginning in the 1920s and that by 1950 the number of carp in Malheur Lake had reached critical levels. The exact mechanism of how the explosion in carp numbers isolated the Blitzen redband from their closest relatives in Silver Creek and the Silvies River has not been explained. However, modern scientific research has shown that the Blitzen redband trout are unique, both in their physical characteristics and their genetic makeup. Another distinguishing aspect of the natural history of the Blitzen redband trout is that they utilize two distinct reproductive strategies; where the riverbed provides adequate gravel and oxygenated water, fish can live and reproduce in the same location year round, but a significant portion of the population migrates long distances within the river course in order to spawn.

The lower portion of the river, from the mouth to the confluence with Bridge Creek, has predominantly sand and silt bedload with inadequate gravel for trout-spawning habitat. The migratory population of Blitzen redband trout are known to inhabit this lower section of the river because it provides superior foraging and growth potential, but in order to reproduce, these migrants move upstream above Page Springs Dam. The Blitzen fish are the only known strain of Great Basin redband trout to exhibit this migratory behavior, and this is one of the stated reasons that Congress designated parts of the Blitzen River as the nation's first trout reserve in 2000.

The big one that got away, the torpedo, was likely one of those migrant redband trout in the Blitzen River. To be as large as it was, it must have lived many years, feasting in the lower river, making annual upstream pilgrimages in the spring, contributing its genetic inheritance to countless offspring and, over the generations, thousands of progeny that are the soul of the river to this day.

URSULA K. LE GUIN

Up in a Cottonwood

i
Who could have for some reason
put a large grey stone
way up in a cottonwood?
Not even on a branch: a twig
holds up that feather boulder
softer than the evening air.

Another deeper in the leaves
turns its silent horns this way,
gazes, shifts the grip
of the mousedeath talons
and softly tells us who.

ii
Indignant indolence.
Wrath gone all downy.
An awful gold round glare
shut halfway to pure contempt.
Birdwatchers.
Someone should remove them.
If they were smaller
If it were evening
I would see to it.
And presently
issue a pellet containing their bones.

iii
Moon cursive
shell curve
of wings in leaves and shadows
soundless, halfseen.

An owl is mostly air.

Who owns the history of the Great Basin? We all do. We all make it, in one way or another. What we know of the ancient history of this region comes in part from the work of archaeologists who examined what can be found of previous occupation of the basin. Greg Bryant recalls his own experiences sifting the sands of the Catlow and Alvord Basins with renowned anthropologist Mel Aikens.

GREG BRYANT

Digging for Universals

The moment you discover a handful of writing, the time of its writing becomes "historic." If we accept this definition, then "prehistory" has a kind of density, with more of it or less of it, in every time and place, depending on available records.

My personal prehistory includes a mostly unrecorded summer, an archaeological expedition in the spectacular deserts and gorges of eastern Oregon in 1979. We extracted the residue of the distant and possibly idyllic lives of prehistoric peoples occupying Steens Mountain as far back as twelve thousand years ago. In that era, water was more abundant in this diverse landscape but, as far as we know, archivists were not.

The scribes of history finally arrived, but rather late: first in the 1930s with Professor Luther Cressman and his small band of young male student laborers. (Luther Cressman can't be recalled without mentioning that he was Margaret Mead's first husband. He was, like Mead, a student of the great cultural leveler and anti-racism campaigner Franz Boas, who launched anthropology in the United States and fought academic support for colonialism. Cressman was trained as a sociologist and a priest but didn't resist the draft into archaeology, because it was obviously just another approach to understanding people.) And later still for our story: dominated by an army of nearly fifty young women and men from three universities in Oregon and Washington, a crazy exercise in infatuation with the past, broader and larger than could possibly be launched today. Both times, these adventures were called a "field school."

The idea of a field school is so helpful that I must stress its importance. It is a healthy solution to an intractable health problem in higher education: any careful and introspective researcher finds it difficult to use the word "teach" without choking a little. How can we fully explain the richness and poorly understood complexities of real research? It's unenlightened to pressure ourselves to reflect upon our experience, cast unearthed and probably incorrect aphorisms and characterizations into textbooks, and then force students to consume them. Instead, let's simply invite them to join the discovery and become colleagues for a season. Let them learn.

For example, when I joined this field school, none of the professors imagined spending the first weeks coping with sneaky treasure hunters who repeatedly breached fences and destroyed excavations untouched since the 1930s. These so-called pot-hunters were after arrowheads and .. . pots. Our attention had attracted the attention of these looters: it would be hard to ignore the helicopters that delivered the cyclone fences. In a classroom, no professor could convey all possible approaches to decontaminating a site under such an active assault. And there was no need. Through the cooperative effort of site repair, students discovered the desired high standards.

The effect of a field school is profound. But teaching and working at the same time is still difficult. Field school directors need to be community organizers, and they tend toward a self-sacrificing commitment to training the next generation of researchers. Mel Aikens led comprehensive digs in deserts for decades and built bridges between archaeologists in the United States and Japan. He served as the head of the University of Oregon anthropology department that Cressman had founded. University of Washington professor Don Grayson is a paleobiologist and evolutionary theorist with a prodigious memory, and his students could reliably identify hundreds of animals from mere scraps of bone. Pete Mehringer Jr. (whose father was an Olympic gold medalist in wrestling) is a paleo-botanist and palynologist who led us to extract pollen strata in cores from the bottom of ice-cold mountain lakes, to initiate the difficult process of uncovering entire plant ecologies. He was extremely patient with students fumbling around on his small, field-built water platforms piled high with custom scaffolding.

The original plan of our summertime adventure—even before the pot-hunters intervened—was ambitious and multidisciplinary, and it required a robust team. We needed to overcome a century-old backlog of untested assumptions about northern Great Basin prehistoric peoples.

The expeditions in the 1930s were guided by empathy and intuition. That's a good place to start: perhaps the only one. But intuition provides no more than a prologue in the natural sciences, because nature, even our own nature, rarely agrees with our instinct, and many of our assumptions become comical, upon examination. Take our earlier example of "pre-history," an academic-sounding but ultimately silly idea. The proposed distinction dissolves when we simply admit that we are animals—so all of our past is natural history.

Cressman provided interesting theories, radiocarbon-dateable spec-imens, and artifacts with context: small clues to the region's natural his-tory. He discovered the world's oldest shoes and pushed back the known beginnings of Northwest human occupation. His work was a little rough, but he conclusively demonstrated that Northwest natural history was worth serious study.

Our new seriousness in 1979 demanded extensive random sampling of a vast area to help identify biases in these intuitive theories of human habitation. It was very ambitious, and Cressman, who came to visit, was pleased with the direction. It resonated with Boas' famous counsel to sci-entific investigators, to work to eliminate their cultural presumptions.

This sampling couldn't be completely random, of course. All data is retrieved by the questions, assumptions, limitations, and equipment that you carry with you. We do our best to identify our human predilections and shortcomings. The goal of natural science is not omniscience. Just better theories.

Luckily, random sampling creates an exciting life for student workers.

We never knew where we'd go. Or what we'd do. Or with whom. We might dig a hole, climb a cliff, sift for bones, row across a lake, carefully separate the undisturbed strata from the packrat middens, or prepare a layer of photogenic tephra from the eruption of Mount Mazama . . . this heady variety compensated for the lack of archaeological treasure. For an expedition of this nature, where so little remains of ancient habitat, the goal cannot include 'spectacular discoveries'—a distracting co-conspirator of intuitive archaeology. Instead, we want a carefully constructed, deep panorama of the natural history in question. And we want to improve our methods. The students were aware of these epistemological difficulties and were happy to play the role of human scattershot.

But all of this seemed whimsical to the modern denizens of eastern Oregon, our 'wild west' neighbors, to whom we'd occasionally and enthusiastically explain our rationale, and defend our sanity, over an afternoon milkshake at the general store in the tiny town of Fields. They certainly sympathized with our desire to know the past. Generally, people who live far from 'civilization' are keen local historians. They also deeply appreciate the prodigious feats of memorization and reconstruction common to field archaeologists, whose attention to detail uncovers the puzzles that lead to serious scientific investigation. So we helped the locals understand the importance of the Pleistocene. This understanding became a regional consensus, partly achieved through peer pressure, since we easily tripled the population of the immediate area with our creek-side village of dozens of tents.

Although we conquered the region, it was painful to acclimatize to the desert. The daily heat could reach 40 Celsius (104 Fahrenheit). We'd get up early to avoid the late afternoon boil. But not every challenge was susceptible to planning, since fortune dropped us into environments that no cautious local person would visit—unless they were chasing stray sheep.

Flocks of students stretched across the summer inhospitalities of desert lakebeds in the Alvord and Catlow Valleys, walking for miles in huge transect formations. We'd call out "flake" whenever we saw obsidian or chert flakes, which were evidence of human occupation. We'd all stop, collect, record, and then resume transecting. If there were innumerable flakes, we'd mark the spot as a potential site for a later mapping survey—a harder, hotter, more-focused effort. Plentiful birds from the Malheur

Mel Aikens and a student sifting the earth of Harney County. Photo by Greg Bryant.

National Wildlife Refuge, just up the road, circled and mocked us by mimicking "flake!" as they zoomed by. Vultures also came, hoping that we might be lost and dying.

Personally, in this extreme environment, I felt free to dress quite eccentrically. I wore a Japanese karate *dogi*—a thick white canvas outfit, loose to the skin and hypothetically reflective—and a terry cloth hat that I could pour water over. I'm not sure my preparations for the unanticipated were successful: white clothing is difficult to keep white, over months of camping. I was still too hot. And I looked odd and scruffy.

Destiny's statistical sampling machine sent a handful of dusty young students for a week to a distant, abandoned high plateau ranch, sitting on steep cliffs overlooking Catlow Valley—an area called Lauserica. We surveyed the flanks of a randomly chosen hillside. The scene was uncommonly beautiful, surrounded by natural fields of short, sharp-to-the-touch mosses, which could easily be mistaken for lush, landscaped lawns. Long-abandoned stone buildings sat on the plateau, which were scenic, but not inviting, so we erected a small one-pole army tent and piled in for some surprisingly cold nights.

One of those nights, an endless, apocalyptic storm blew through, with an abundant supply of monsoon rain, wind, and lightning. We braced against this for hours and hours. We should have been killed. We were at the highest point, by thousands of feet, and our tent had a conspicuous, thick, lightning-friendly metal rod running down its center. We couldn't go outside, since the tent would get washed or blown off the mountain without our weight. We pressed back against the soaking wet walls, as far as possible from our cast iron tentpole, which became electromagnetically possessed, vibrating violently like an off-kilter washing machine. The level of static electricity made even our damp hair stand on end. Nature had saturated our evening with terrific educational opportunities.

The summer provided countless smaller learning moments for everyone. We had an excellent camp chef who required a team of students to wash pots and dishes several times a day. One evening this crew was a bit rushed, and didn't completely rinse off the soap. Almost everyone became ill, including, in my stretched memory, some distinguished elderly visitors. Perhaps Cressman. This kind of poisoning was a revelation to the teenagers involved.

Back at the main camp, which straddled a cool creek, there was a large field office tent dedicated to the labelling of samples, specimens, and artifacts. If you were bordering on heatstroke, you could request a week of this administrative work, which provided a wonderful chance to take leisurely lunches, welcome visiting scholars, and engage the backlog of community chores: patching tents, fixing latrines and showers, clearing brush, or building exciting amenities.

In the labeling tent, everyone threw their music cassettes into a pile to play during the long hours of work, since no radio signal reached the area. Surprisingly, we developed a shared musical taste. A touch of classical, some newgrass, some jazz, and lots of folk rock. When there were enough musicians at main camp, they jammed bluegrass, appropriately enough.

The lab tent housed a kind of field library. Mostly maps and technical books, but also a corner of magazines, journals, field guides, conference proceedings, fiction, and science essays. This kind of "lab library" holds a special resonance for me: a humane and civilized hangout in a sagebrush and alkaline landscape, available at any time. Since culture is within the individual, and emerges through shared experience, we began to develop our particular culture, being so close and sharing so much, with no break.

We discussed great ideas of the day. What else was there to do? We now had time to reflect upon, digest, and consider those ideas and questions that accumulate during the school year, but become forgotten over a summer. This was perfect—we were still in school, in the sense that we had colleagues, but we were on a break from being crammed with facts. We could breathe. We had time to think and explore. We had older folks around who were happy to entertain ideas. It felt more like real science, and real rationality, than our pressured time at school.

I remember lively nighttime discussions about evolutionary biology, attended also by a variety of lizards, crickets, sparrows, and mice. Our distance from civilization gave us the freedom to highlight misguided trends in scientific thought that might seem appealing but were overly simple: blank slates, behaviorism, positivism, extremist selectionism, the dogmas of molecular biology, and the already unraveling modern synthesis of evolutionary biology. We loved poking fun at shaky technical definitions that we'd learned in school. Somehow these discussions became like confessionals—people poured out their doubts about human endeavors amidst the reality of camping in nature, and supported each other in the hope that we could do better.

I was under the impression that these curious discussions left an impression with the directors, who remembered me whenever I contacted them, even decades later. After all, I was a computer scientist, and only an anthropological dilettante. I never planned to become an archaeologist. I've interacted with anthropologists my whole life—including Margaret Mead, who pulled me into some kind of multicultural experiment with children in the 1960s in a strange room with carpets on the walls behind the insect zoo at the American Museum of Natural History, where I took classes as a child.

But apparently my keen mind was not my most memorable quality for others at the camp. I had a beer with one of the directors nearly forty years later, who said, "Do you know why I remember you? You shared a tent with three female students for a month. There was a lot of gossip. Everyone wondered what was going on."

I wasn't alone: if you wake college students at 6 a.m., that doesn't necessarily keep them from partying at night. Nor does it make them obedient. The field school directors regularly used tongue-in-cheek exclamations like 'mutiny!' when we didn't behave, grabbing hold of our own time when work was done. This behavior was partly a consequence of the improved gender-balance in field archaeology, which apparently had begun to emerge at the time. Margaret Mead, after all, was the most famous anthropologist in history. Clearly gender-balance is good for the sciences. And it made the collective ideas and experiences of the field-school workers at least twice as rich.

So what did we discover in our unbiased wanderings? A great deal of data was collected, and the analysis showed that human intuition hadn't done too badly. People tend to go where you think they will, if you've dedicated a few decades to a multidisciplinary reconstruction of their long-gone climates and ecologies, so that you can get a sense of what it's like to step into their shoes.

We are the same human species. So it should be no surprise that, to a great extent, with many caveats, the best tool you possess for studying ancient people is *yourself*, since you empathize with the same feelings and motivations, and understand the same ideas.

The problem is that, from the point of view of the natural sciences, we can use our internal "human meters" to do useful investigations into the lives of people—but we really don't know what humans are. We recognize human activity, but we couldn't explain it to an alien or a machine. In that sense, we don't know ourselves. This is normal in natural science— take something that everyone thinks they know, and then you realize that it's actually a complete mystery. Once you begin to investigate this mystery, you don't get answers, you only get occasional insights. And every moment of enlightenment is like getting to the top of a mountain, where you discover new mountain ranges that you need to climb. It is this perpetual mystery that drives science—otherwise we would simply say that we know everything, or that we can explain anything—which is an anti-scientific attitude sometimes known as scientism.

Strangely, if you want answers to universal mysteries, you might be attracted to natural science, but unless you slow down, become deeply humble, and begin to see the limits of the human mind, you won't make any progress. And real progress will take a great deal of work, which you cannot do alone. Luckily, the joy of discovery during collaboration provides its own rewards. Anyone who is exposed to it will never get enough.

DAVID HEDGES

Alvord Desert Stars

Flat on our backs, warm in our double bag
beneath the Alvord Desert's lavish dome,
we tune to nearby dune and distant crag,
the sounds of all who call this landscape home—
the flap of bats, the whir of great horned owls,
the slithering of skinks and rattlesnakes,
the scritch and scratch of scuttling voles, the howls
and yips a pack of skulking coyotes makes.

Invited here to celebrate the night
swayed by the music of the spheres, the play
of Pleiades, we sate our appetite
for space by swallowing the Milky Way.
Who but two groupies camped in sand and sage
would know the password to the door backstage?

What does it mean to be truly engaged with a place like the Harney Basin? Ultimately it means recognizing that the people who live there are doing so on purpose. They are part of the web, the pattern of life. Their needs and choices matter. The conversation between visitor and resident goes on all the time, but has been very visible in recent years as tourist activity has expanded into the dry parts of the region and, in January 2016 in particular, with the Bundy occupation of Malheur National Wildlife Refuge headquarters. Know these experiences with Ellen Waterston, who is there on purpose, too.

ELLEN WATERSTON

High Centered

First of all, it's "Oreygun," not "Orahgone." And it's "Malhyure" out here. Not the French pronunciation of "malheur," although the French trappers that came through Oregon's high desert in 1819 were plenty unhappy. Once they left the stands of Ponderosa in the mountains and entered the desert, nothing went right. Their cached beaver pelts were snatched by Indians, there was little water, no shelter, no shade. It didn't go much better for the Hawaiian trappers, also working for the North West Company, who came up missing the same year in the farthest southeastern corner of the state, and after whom the stunningly beautiful Owyhee River and Canyon Lands were named, that being the standard spelling of Hawaii at the time.

Speaking of names, Oregon's Outback, the sage steppe, the empty quarter, the cold desert, the back of beyond, cowboy country, the nothing-but-nothing, the sagebrush ocean, the great basin, the great sandy desert, the rolling sage plain, the Artemisia desert all refer to the same thing: the high desert. Since the nineteenth century, us "settlers" have tried to name this place, and thereby, as is the fancy of settlers, to lay claim to it. But the enduring fascination of the high desert, and the reason its survival as a wild place is seen as vital by so many, may well lie in the fact that this vast open can't quite be named. It stays always one step ahead of the namers, luring us who would try deeper and deeper into its embrace. "Here" says Karen Shepherd, "it is possible to see a hawk and believe in magic."

People definitely get kind of Carlos Castaneda-esque about this high desert. They also get real. That a rancher hangs a coyote hide on a fence doesn't mean the rancher is angry at the government, as author Nancy Langston speculated in a *New York Times* piece. It means the rancher is angry at the coyote. Sometimes a cigar *is* just a cigar. The coyote ate the rancher's newborn livestock. "Makes a person mad," states a rancher in typically understated fashion. The only indication of a stronger emotion: the force behind the spit of chewing tobacco he sends to the ground. As far as the rancher is concerned, the dead coyote draped over the barbed wire fence murdered, robbed, ate a hole in his wallet. This brief pronunciation and cultural guide matters. Simply stated, we have to remove our cultural and class filters to have the necessary conversation about this place, and about all the people who love it in their unique and incompatible ways.

Those who have never been to Oregon imagine the whole state rainy and green, like Portland or Seattle, believe that the "Portlandia" culture made popular by the sketch comedy television series culturally characterizes all of the ninety-eight thousand square miles of this northwestern wonderland. In fact, three-quarters of the state is dry, separated from "the valley," as the western portion is referred to, by the majestic Cascade mountains, all dormant volcanoes, at least for now. They block the rains from coming east, keep the high desert the high desert. Where I live, in Bend, Oregon, at the foot of the Cascades on the eastern side, the average annual rainfall is twelve inches a year. As one old-timer said: "Remember that time it rained forty days and forty nights? We got an inch and a half in eastern Oregon." It's a part of the world where evaporation exceeds precipitation literally and metaphorically, giving back more than it receives. It's a desert that doesn't get the credit it deserves for its generosity.

A year ago, last April, I drove the 130 miles east and south from Bend, located roughly in the middle of the state, to Burns to attend the Harney County Migratory Bird Festival, a favorite annual event of mine. It felt good to get away from Bend's increasingly California-esque culture. A former lumber-mill town, Bend is now ultra-chic, latte'd, churning with construction and growth, teeming with self-aware, forty-something bio and high-tech CEOs. It is one of the fastest growing communities in the United States. It boasts a populace remarkably unaware of the desert that surrounds them. Perhaps that's good news for the desert.

Lucky for me it's only a matter of driving twenty miles east and I am reunited with what has become my reassurance that all is right with the world: vast sagebrush flats, the echo of what used to be ocean bottom, flanked by escarpments and buttes, gnarled juniper forests, scrub sage, basalt canyons carved by ancient rivers. Other than power lines, and perhaps the distant silhouette of a barn or ranch house, nothing to interrupt the view. Along Highway 20 between Bend and Burns, if you stop by the side of the road in the spring the loudest sound is the buzzing of a fly. Artist Robert Dahl once placed a cheesy aluminum folding chair with nylon webbing in the middle of Highway 20 and sat down for the ultimate selfie and existential Christmas card, nothingness ahead, nothingness on either side, nothing to recommend going in any direction . . . or not to.

Closer to Burns the palette changes from the muted browns, grays, and ochres of the sage to bright green, evidence of spring melt and a water table that sits just below the surface of the miles and miles of pancake-flat fields. Dramatically framing them to the west is the 9,733-foot, snow-capped Steens Mountain, its southernmost side a dramatic escarpment that plummets into the Alvord Desert before sliding into base in Nevada. Burns ranch houses built on these seasonally soggy, rice-paddy-like flats don't have basements. Abandoned homesteads and barns shrug their way to the earth as their underpinnings rot. The spring runoff in this land-locked basin creates perfect habitat for birds . . . and the word has spread. The area is part of the migratory path for a huge variety of large- and small-winged victories. Birders with binoculars cruise along the dykes that frame fields of hay, alfalfa, and Timothy grass, training their eyes on yellow-headed blackbirds, bitterns, meadowlarks, mergansers, egrets, and willets. Visitors learn to return the favor of an index finger lifted off the steering wheel by the rancher as they pass his oncoming pickup, his stock dog leaning into the wind, teetering on bales of hay stacked in the bed of the truck. It feels like acceptance into the fraternity of those who work the land for a living. It used to be most of us could recall a relative who farmed or ranched. Not so much anymore.

What started in 1981 in the town's grange hall, the Migratory Bird Festival now locates activities all over Burns and at favorite viewpoints within the 187,000 acres of the Malheur National Wildlife Refuge with bird talks and guided tours held within the refuge and on adjacent ranches. You're likely to see flocks of snow geese lifting off the greening meadows like bed sheets flapping in the wind, clusters of avocets, phalaropes, armadas of pelicans, snipes probing the irrigated fields for food, sandhill cranes looking as regal and prehistoric as they are, their ungainly squawk matching their ungainly stride. What people come to observe and exalt is beautiful, glorious, fragile.

On Saturday night of the festival that year, a dinner was held at the Harney County Fairgrounds. There looked to be two hundred people in attendance. More? In any case, a record-breaking turnout, according to organizers. Rectangular plastic banquet tables were decorated with rough-hewn barn-wood boxes made by a local high-school student and filled with wild flowers. Crude paintings of birds, also by students, were on display to be auctioned as well as raffle items from carved ducks to horsehair bracelets to homemade apple butter crafted by local artists and cooks. The gregarious organizer, president of the Burns Chamber of Commerce (considering all the empty storefronts in town, a triumph of hope) orchestrated the evening as she called out raffle winners, waved to friends, introduced speakers. The dinner was prepared by members of the local Mennonite community. Between the main course and dessert, the Mennonite men and boys in their pressed white shirts, the women and girls in their long skirts and small bonnets, came out of the kitchen and lined up next to the toiling coffee pots to sing in the purest of harmonies: "When hay is fresh and new, all my praise to You. When hay is fresh and new, all my praise to You."

Presentations featured a talk about sage grouse habitat and the prospect of the bird being federally protected, a controversial topic among ranchers who feared the designation of the sage grouse as an endangered species would affect their grazing permits and, therefore, their livelihood. For the time being, an uneasy peace had been negotiated between government land-use agencies and private landowners who went to work and successfully created more habitat for the bird. The next talk, by the wife of a local rancher, informed the city folk in attendance about what happens on ranches in the spring of the year—calving, weaning, haying—and then, clearly off-message, she reared up and unabashedly stated that, given all the problems in her community lately, she wanted to let her community law-enforcement officials and the local government land-management agencies know she supported them. Maybe all ranchers didn't, but she did. Most of us, city folks and ranchers alike, knew what she was referring to but none was inclined to give it any purchase. Nope. If the noisy, slightly nervous chatter was any indication, tonight the crowd was clearly eager for a time-out from recent controversies, a night out. Strangers introduced themselves, ranchers and visitors applauded anything and everything, knocking their water glasses over onto the decorative paper doilies, into their whipped cream and fruit salad. A good time.

My drive to the bird festival that weekend not only took me across an ancient ocean bed ruggedly framed by exquisite small canyons but also paralleled sections of what was, in 2012, designated as the Oregon Desert Trail. The Oregon Natural Desert Association, based in Bend, plotted and got approved the seven-hundred-fifty-mile trail in 2012. It starts at the Oregon Badlands Wilderness preserve outside of Bend and continues to the southeastern Oregon canyon lands that flank the Owyhee River, taking pains to stay on public lands the whole way.

I moved from New England to the high desert to ranch four decades ago. Though I now live "in town," my love of this hardscrabble outback still informs my every day. So no surprise that this new trail spoke to me. No longer actively ranching, the notion of it lured me back out into the desert. I greedily walked sections of the trail. I made plans to walk more. I took note of what I saw, of conversations with those I encountered, became increasingly interested in the conflicting points of view about re-purposing open areas of public land. I prided myself that in so many ways I already knew the players: ranchers, Bureau of Land Management and Fish and Wildlife employees, school teachers in rural schoolhouses, merchants in remote outposts, Native Americans, law enforcement officials who years before had waved me on, despite my excessive speed, as I made my way along the desolate Highway 20 back to our ranch with a station wagon full of fussy infants and sacks of groceries.

At the Migratory Bird Festival dinner, I asked my tablemates their thoughts about the Oregon Natural Desert Association's effort to punch a trail through this wide-open, tumble-dry high desert. As they finished their salads and passed around the fresh-baked rolls, I posited my latest idea: the trail is as long and circuitous as it is not only to lead trekkers through some of the most scenic, and heretofore unexplored, areas of the high desert but also because it dares not stray off public lands lest risking conflicts with private landowners. What about the not-so-random course of this high desert *camino?* What about the key concerns facing this sagebrush ocean that it touches on as it meanders from the north to the southeast: protection of sacred Native American ground, protection of habitat for endangered species, elimination of "predators," "wild" horse protection, grazing "rights" for livestock, hunting "rights," water "rights," demand for recreational land for motorized vehicles, demand for land for low-impact recreational uses? It struck me, I related, that these issues meet head-on at various intersections along the trail. Solutions that work for all seemed elusive, charged, complicated—but do exist. How, to me, the Oregon Trail, as it zig and zags to avoid privately held tracts, is a powerful metaphor for all the land-use issues facing not just southeastern Oregon but all the ranching West.

As my mashed potatoes and roast beef got cold and my audience restless, I went on (and on) about the broader philosophical musings I felt the trail excites as suggested by the insinuating and contradictory "rights" various groups and users claim. What is wild? Who says grazing is a right? Who says it isn't? What is the highest best use of public lands? According to whom? Whose version of the "story" is most compelling, best "marketed," is influencing policy decisions? Is a designated trail a good thing, a natural thing . . . or an insult, an intrusion, a disruption to a landscape, to "native" flora and fauna? Is the trail itself the imposition of a particular and stylized narrative? "Seems like," replied one, "a passionate love of the same place isn't a predictor for common solutions. Pass the coffee and the cream and sugar."

I'd come to the Migratory Bird Festival this time with not only my bird book in hand, but also walking sticks. My plan was, before heading back to Bend, to explore sections of the Oregon Desert Trail I hadn't explored that wind through Harney County. More specifically the Malheur National Wildlife Refuge. But this time was different. Most of the birding tours sold out for the first time in the thirty-four-year history of the festival. The Saturday night banquet was at capacity. Local motels were full. Because curiosity killed the cat. Because Burns, Oregon, is the county seat of Harney County where the Malheur Wildlife Refuge Occupation took place in January and February 2016. It was now April. Ammon Bundy and his band had left the refuge only two months before. The buildings they occupied on the refuge and portions of the refuge itself were still closed to the public. Robert Lavoy Finicum was dead. Damage to land and Native American artifacts and burial grounds was still being assessed. Burns, overwhelmed by news teams, was now on the map. The occupation had identified a new 1 percent . . . those in the nation who had actually *heard* of Harney County, the refuge, and Burns, Oregon. But, United States of America, ignore what took place there at your peril.

In light of the forty-one-day occupation, my tidy idea of the Oregon Desert Trail as a vehicle for finding common ground on important issues was rendered a nursery rhyme, la, la, a polite conversation about land-use conflicts. The trail—a contrivance of my making to daisy-chain the perspectives of those who want to harvest natural resources and those who want to protect land for various recreational and environmental reasons. Any reasonable discussion about land-use policy options now turned into a shouting match between, for starters, those who wanted no government intrusion and those who understood the benefits of government involvement and collaboration. And since the Bundy occupation, militias have gone public, brother has remained armed against brother, wrong information has been embraced as fact, corroborated facts as fake news. How armed and dangerous we are! How blunt an instrument our thinking has become. How very afraid we are. How misappropriated by Bundy-style thinkers is the United States constitution, never mind God. How misunderstood the laws affecting land-use and, well, everything if one believes the occupiers. And tragically many do.

Seemingly overnight this unknown region of the United States became the poster child not only for land-use and conservation issues but also for the angry, gun-toting, militia-organizing, and disenfranchised who came to define the 2016 presidential election, dramatically reframing America's conversation. This demographic, like this area of the United States, is no longer unknown, uncharted. The damage caused by the failure of those who see themselves as educated, informed, and at the helm of this nation to acknowledge and engage the rural, white, working class is incalculable. This failure has trivialized the important message the cursive script of the Oregon Desert Trail inscribes across southeastern Oregon. It risks undermining the Oregon Desert Trail's potential to maybe, just maybe, create a path to reconciliation and collaboration regarding land-use and related cultural and lifestyle issues in the region. It thwarts it as a national model that could be applied in other regions, could be held up against the light of many other similar problems across the United States. Worst of all, this failure in national leadership has so disturbed the social soil that the toxic dust of unrest and foment released into the atmosphere the nation may not be able to withstand.

"When hay is fresh and new, all my praise to You. When hay is fresh and new, all my praise to You."

ADA HASTINGS HEDGES

Wild Geese

In dark flight beating south they made
An etching thin and high—
I watched them in the early dusk
Go down the desert sky.

They left an arc of loneliness
To widen east and west,
An edge more piercing to the wind,
And winter in my breast.

The Malheur of heat and mosquitos is the image many people have of the refuge. The cross-flit of thousands of yellow warblers; orioles whooping in cottonwoods and a blizzard of chattering, particolored swallows is all that many of us ever see. And it's a lot. Yet there is another Malheur, of snow and rough-legged hawks, of tiny drifts of boreal finches, of immense quiet. This is the Malheur that Noah Strycker brings us, from one of his many winter visits to the region.

NOAH K. STRYCKER

Malheur in Winter

2017

A few years ago, at dawn on an early winter's day, my dad and I were driving out of the Malheur Field Station when we noticed something on top of a power pole.

"Great horned owl," my dad said, and I mumbled agreement.

The shape was round and fluffy, grayish brown, and it had two distinct ear tufts. Having seen my share of great horneds on countless trips to southeast Oregon, I hardly bothered a second glance—but I should have known better than to take anything for granted at Malheur. As we passed under the power pole, my dad hit the brakes and exclaimed, "Whoa, it's a bobcat!"

We eased a hundred yards down the road and gingerly opened the car doors, angling for a good view. The bobcat didn't budge. On its high perch, surrounded by sagebrush, it was safe and seemed to enjoy the early slanting rays of sunshine.

Around us, the high desert was quiet. Winter brings a sweeping peace to Malheur, the priceless solitude that is usually reserved for inaccessible wilderness. A person fills more room in wide-open spaces, and it doesn't take many fair-weather tourists for Malheur to get crowded. In winter, when hardly anyone visits, the landscape exudes meditative calm.

A deep chill had settled in overnight, and this bobcat curled itself into a tight ball, peering down at us with evident curiosity.

"You never know what's around the next corner," my dad murmured with appreciation as he snapped a photo. We watched the cat for a couple of minutes before leaving it to its sunrise vigil, and continued down the Center Patrol Road to see what else the day might bring.

For years now, my dad and I have made a near-annual wintertime pilgrimage to Malheur. We also go in other seasons—each has its attractions—but winter stands out. Our tradition started when, fresh out of high school, I spent a fall season volunteering at the wildlife refuge. Having decided to defer college for a year, I called to ask if I could help the biologists with their work. They promptly set me up in a three-bedroom house at headquarters, loaned me a pickup truck, and dispatched me for bird surveys and fencing projects. I hung around the office, staffed the visitor center, and went birding every day from September through November.

That fall, I watched the seasons change in increments. The cottonwood and aspen leaves flamed out, and then the nights turned brisk. The first snow fell on Halloween, dusting headquarters in several inches of light powder; that same day, thousands of snow geese and tundra swans streamed overhead, aiming south, in continuous flocks.

By the time I departed in mid-November, the visitor center was virtually unvisited—most days, nobody stopped by. I packed up to spend the rest of my gap year in Taiwan, Mexico, and Panama before starting college the following spring. But I often thought about those tranquil days at Malheur and wondered what it was like when winter really took hold. The following year, my dad and I planned a long weekend at the field station in January. We've been regular winter migrants ever since.

Midwinter is not the time to see a ton of birds. A few hardy species remain year-round, sticking it out through the most desolate conditions: golden eagles, common ravens, and canyon wrens haunt the rimrock, and the occasional ruby-crowned kinglet flits in bare willows. But minimalism is itself a virtue, and the cold months at Malheur present a chance to set aside the usual distractions. When a landscape is laid bare, so, too, is the life within it.

Some birds, such as owls, are easier to find in midwinter. Take a slow January drive down the Center Patrol Road, eyeballing each leafless cottonwood tree and willow thicket, and you'll invariably spot one—most likely a great horned, though with patience you might discover a placid barn or even a snoozing long-eared. Without layers of foliage, owls have nowhere to hide.

In the high desert, winter draws back the curtain, unmasks the actors, and simplifies the plot lines. Nests from previous seasons reveal themselves after the leaves drop, reminders of birds that have since flown thousands of miles to warmer climes. The birds that stay tend to be approachable in winter, when they are more preoccupied with warmth and food than avoiding predators.

Birding is also, in a way, much more civilized when the sun rises late and sets early. In December, unlike May, it's unnecessary to rise at 4:30 a.m. to catch the early birds. You can sleep in, grab a cozy mug of something hot, and venture out without missing a thing. After a day in the field, you may return to a long, relaxing evening of editing photos and thumbing field guides.

For me, Malheur will always be special. Over the years, I made my way through college and then around the world on birdwatching projects, returning home to Oregon. My dad and I still make our annual wintertime journey to the place we've explored so many times together. It's now been fifteen years since our first pilgrimage, and every visit brings something new. These days, the trips also offer precious time to catch up between other adventures.

People and jobs may come and go, but Malheur, and its birds, have an enduring quality best appreciated in winter. When the snow falls, the thermometer drops to near zero, and fog freezes on the sage, my dad and I will pack up the car, head over the mountains, and see what awaits in the high desert.

Malheur can overload the senses of the average five-day visitor. So much flooding in and so much that is new. For college student Thomas Meinzen, steeping in the air and water of the refuge for an entire summer was a modern equivalent of Tom McAllister's visit of 1942. Meinzen lets us experience the process of taking in the daily detail of Malheur and placing himself within this immensity of space and life.

THOMAS C. MEINZEN

My Infinite Summer

The morning after the forty-one-day Bundy occupation of Malheur came to an end, I got a phone call. Yes, the summer internship is still going to happen, I was told. And I'd been picked for the job. Three months later my dad and I drove over from Eugene, winding up through fern-cloaked slopes, among the scarred trunks of pines, and down into the deep wide open of eastern Oregon. The shine of our red Prius beamed incongruously, a wayward tropical tanager in the high desert world of earth tones, pastel blues, and soft greens.

Passing south of Burns, the scraping calls of yellow-headed blackbirds brought me back to my first trip to Malheur, six years prior. I remembered gaping at flocks of ibis gliding across the marshes, staring down willets on roadside fenceposts, and pleading to stay longer. Now here I was, at last, with all the time in the world. Well, two months—a small eternity for a nineteen-year-old.

We veered east to climb Wright's Point, an ancient river of extruded lava snaking like a fortress wall to divide Malheur from the lights of its nearest cities. Swinging over the escarpment, central Harney County stretched out before us, a sunstruck quilt of cloud shadow and sagebrush, twinkling with the reds and golds of blooming hopsage. I breathed in and smiled.

Four burrowing owls glared at us from fence posts as we rolled down the bleached highway toward Sodhouse Lane. Their narrowed yellow eyes seemed to catch my own and hold them, and I turned in my seat to follow their receding forms into speckdom when we passed by. Finally, we turned down Sodhouse, a faded asphalt track cutting through wetlands crackling with blackbirds. My first nighthawk of the year passed in front of us, its long graceful wings sweeping over the road like the intake of breath before a deep sigh. Over the marshes, the air was swarming with life. Malheur. Paradise—with a large side of mosquitoes.

We left Sodhouse and headed down a washboard gravel road, the dust quickly dulling our car to a more reasonable rosy brown. I gazed around with anticipation, each roadside meadowlark and sage thrasher made more significant with the thrilling thought that this would be my drive to work for the next eight weeks. A pair of quail parents with eleven chicks skittered across the road as we turned into the broken gravel lot of Malheur Field Station: my home for the summer.

The field station, an old federal conservation camp complex, nestles between two volcanic buttes that rise in sharp relief against the surrounding expanse of sagebrush. But for a few Russian olives, the station directors have deferred to natural vegetation on the grounds. The *Artemisia* and rabbitbrush around the old sun-stained buildings hum with life. Nighthawks line the low fences and gangs of blackbirds glide over from the slough a half-mile to the east. Jackrabbits and cottontails spring tentatively through the shrubs and come nightfall, kangaroo rats and deer mice dance across the station's moonlit gravel lanes.

When I moved into Owl West, my dorm building, I quickly unplugged the old thrumming oven—the better to hear the morning meadowlarks. The next day, I filled Owl West's cupboards with the canned soup and mac and cheese I'd brought, set my alarm for 3:30 a.m. (survey work began before dawn), laced up my boots, and set out to explore.

That first exploration and those that followed turned up some wonderful surprises. A family of great horned owls roosted in the Russian olives by the abandoned basketball court, the slate-gray male sporting a pair of toweringly tall ear tufts. A single secretive pair of black-throated sparrows scraped together a living in the hopsage meadow on the south butte. Across the station, a couple of western kingbirds raised a family in the end of a building gutter—a testament to Malheur's dependable aridity.

Wildlife became a calendar of sorts for the passage of summer at the field station. In mid-June, families of Say's phoebes queued up along the station's fences, their salmon-tinged bellies bright against the weathered gray wood. When tens of thousands of clear-winged grasshoppers swarmed the station at the month's end, the phoebes feasted in quiet reverie, enjoying the momentary bounty of this traveling buffet. The grasshoppers coated the lot outside my window in swirling mustard yellow, laying eggs in the hot gravel and filling the air with a whirring, churring, whispering. This too shall pass, they seemed to say.

Soon enough, the phoebes were once again searching far and wide for smaller fare. Their plaintive *pee-ur*s echoed against the peeling paint and settled into the empty desert air.

I remember reading in Kathleen Dean Moore's *Holdfast* a quote from a friend of hers, that if eternal life exists, it must be in depth, not in length. For me, Malheur was saturated with moments of such eternal depth. The barely perceptible song of a poorwill in the first purplings of dusk . . . the pre-dawn symphony of robins and kingbirds under a cathedral of stars . . . the bugles of cranes rising unseen from behind willow breaks sparkling with yellow warblers.

Of course, my summer at Malheur also had its moments of seemingly infinite length. Tallying thousands of mallard, pintail, and gadwall at Boca Lake; examining leaf after leaf of milkweed in an often-fruitless search for monarch eggs; quiet afternoons of hot dust and unbroken blue; nights with two mosquitoes beside my pillow I couldn't quite seem to catch. Time seemed more creative at Malheur, taking flight with the restless shorebirds, buzzing in circles of day and night like my blood-craving companions, or seeping on into the endless azure as slowly as the sagebrush growing outside my window.

In an effort to cultivate a bodily rhythm among pre-dawn surveys, occasional five-hour afternoon naps, and this creative Malheur time, I took to running up to the south butte's summit every day at sunset. A rough trail snaked from Owl West beyond the butte, corkscrewing up its southeastern face to the gravelly top, scraggled with hopsage and rabbit-brush. If I timed my run perfectly, I would climb the butte in shadow, then round the summit and be struck full on by a wall of golden light—a burst of photovoltaic energy to power my final panting strides.

At the top, I would stand, blood pulsing behind my eyes, feeling the incredible, improbable life within me. And even more, around me, independent of me, an overwhelmingly variety of other beings beating into the silence. Rabbitbrush peeling back sepals, petals, thrusting stamens heavenward; lichens inching glacially across stones; snakes, coyotes, jackrabbits calculating behind ebony pupils the unwritten formulas of predator and prey; roots stretching into the earth; everything splitting into a million wild indefinable parts.

At the top of the butte at sunset, I was always breathless.

In early July, nighthawks began lining up in dozens, perching lengthwise along the low wooden fences of the field station. When disturbed, their wonderful peenting calls would echo off the building walls as the cryptic birds arose to find quieter perches. Every other day after work, I'd walk around and count them, recording their cardinal orientation and the height at which they roosted, along with the temperature and wind speed. Over time, patterns emerged: on hot and less windy days, they crowded the wires high above; cooler, windier weather saw them lined along structures a few feet above the ground. Presumably, proximity to the ground increased both warmth and wind protection. Perhaps more surprising was the consistency of roosting nighthawks' orientation toward the prevailing wind. On days of high wind speed, nearly every nighthawk on the field station would be turned to face directly into the wind. I surmise that this orientation minimized air friction across their bodies.

Although as many as fifty nighthawks congregated around the station's ample roost sites in the day, come evening the airspace seemed to divide, invisible lines separating the area into the territories of three male nighthawks. One guarded the north butte, another patrolled the valley between and the sage expanse westward, and a third lorded over the south butte.

One particularly glorious evening, I watched the king of the between-space display at sunset. Over a backdrop of sun-sliced, auburn-tinged clouds, this nighthawk climbed to the tips of the last sunrays steadily, gracefully, and then suddenly, pulled his wings skyward and dropped in a steep swooshing stroke like a well-practiced doctor's signature, down, down, DOWN across that riot of deepening sun and carameled cloud like the silent "wow" that you mouth when you're alone and amazed. And maybe you wish you had a reason to say it aloud, but then *boom* comes the torpedo of sound through the free fall and you blink, loneliness forgotten, and then somehow the nighthawk is back, steadily rising, calling, flapping as though it had never become a falling star at all.

I stood there for nearly an hour, the mosquitoes forgotten (although, as I found out the morning after, they did not forget me), watching this nighthawk streak down the sky, seeing how when he had nearly reached the horizon, he would suddenly thrust his wings down, the air pushing against them with a sound like a racecar zooming past, dropped four octaves, arcing him out of his dive and back toward the stars. If I could send someone a gift of raw, elemental beauty, I would send that evening.

In mid-July, Malheur's profusions of floral color ascended. Blooms that had once sparkled among sagebrush flats now broke into yellows and oranges on the rimrock above. The hopsage that had decorated the south butte in early June disappeared into a landscape of faded gray-green. I headed out to the Steens for a weekend, following the flowers.

On the first night at South Steens Campground, a new moon drew me out to a treeless meadow near camp. Here the sky seemed to draw in close, as though it had a secret to share. I spread out on a lichen-rough boulder, breathing in a night sky so black it made a bobolink's face look gray. A river of starlight stretched from east to west, brighter than I'd ever seen it before. Transfixed, I almost missed it the first time: a sudden darkness, deeper even than the spangled sky, passed above me. I held my breath and suddenly the stars winked out, then immediately back into view, as though the heavens themselves had blinked.

I held my breath again; then suddenly, again: out, in. This time, a shape: long wings, a silhouetted round head. Noiselessly, the creature made several more passes, its wings almost brushing my body. Still the silence remained untouched.

Later that night came the thick, dark, contrabass hoot of my mysterious company, gliding across the meadow: a male long-eared owl. The greatest human musician, I thought, could not match this creature's command over sound.

The next morning, I embarked on a full-day exploration up the half-pipe canyon of the Little Blitzen River. Rolling rocky and clear, the river offered a refreshing rush of moisture and color to the desert, harboring clusters of willow and pockets of penstemon and monkeyflower. At the first crossing, clusters of Lorquin's admiral butterflies dabbled for mud minerals, their orange wingtips and zebra stripes flashing in the tree-tossed light. Thistles marched up the banks beyond the river, attended by a spectacular trio of two-tailed swallowtails, each five inches across. Cottonwoods stood rare and regal, their shimmering green leaves appearing lavishly verdant to my sage-acclimated eyes. Moist pockets overflowed with extravagant color: dashes of goldenrod and green spikes of monument plant, cascading bluebells and stately bog orchids.

Hidden among the toes of scraggly ponderosas, the tiny polka-dotted faces of spotted coralroot peeked out through deep shadows. Instead of relying on the sun for energy, these myco-heterotrophic orchids depend upon fungal networks, exchanging nutrients and carbohydrates with the roots of nearby trees. In the heavy heat of July, I too felt energized among the shaded tree roots.

Around noon, I paused on a small island in the creek. Along the stream beside me, western river cruiser dragonflies patrolled through the flickering shadows of wind-touched willows. Two Lorquin's admirals landed on my boots, still soaked from my first river crossing. I stood, eyes open wide like the wings on my shoes, and just then I spotted it: the jet-black, white-splashed wings of something, well . . . different. I hurriedly photographed the butterfly, lying on my belly in the stream to capture the often diagnostic underside of its wings.

Among the hundreds of butterflies that skipped and floated along the Little Blitzen that day, this one was unique. Large and dark, with a startling V of white bars across its outstretched wings, it sparkled in that particular brilliance of rarity—the same brilliance that draws so many birders to Malheur each May, looking for lost birds and long-lost birder friends.

The next day, I headed back up-refuge, the Steens' white crests retreating in my rearview mirror. Upon returning to the field station, I eagerly shared my photos with station directors Lyla and Duncan, who'd hooked me on butterflies a month earlier. They agreed with my tentative identification: a Weidemeyer's admiral, *Limenitis weidemeyerii*, a specialty of the arid southwest, and—according to their thirty-odd years of records—a first for Harney County. I beamed.

My summer at Malheur was sprinkled with such lucky chance encounters as this one. On one early morning bird survey in July, my intern partner, Jesse, and I drove up to a pair of coyote pups, cavorting in the dawn-gray grass of the dike, curious but unafraid of our rumbling Chevy. A week later, an old badger made my sudden acquaintance when we both came round the side of the truck simultaneously—he from the front, me from the back. After a five-second staredown, he seemed to agree that I was indeed the better driver, and he lumbered off into the grass.

Weidemeyer's admiral. Photo by Thomas Meinzen.

Perhaps my most thrilling mammal encounter, however, came while walking across the field station to do my laundry. Most afternoons settled quietly at the station, but one afternoon, quail alarm calls rang out, strident and indignant. Across the old overgrown station playground, I noticed nighthawks, kingbirds, and Say's phoebes all taking flight in the same direction. Odd.

Hurrying forward, I glimpsed a flash of undulating movement through the sage. Then, suddenly, bounding across the open road not ten yards away: a bobcat! It quickly disappeared into the scrub, but then paused, turning suddenly to face me, its face framed by two thick clumps of rabbitbrush. For a long, breathless moment, those powerful, calm, golden eyes met mine. I can only ponder what it was thinking in that moment. *What are YOU doing here?* It seemed to know we were both just visitors.

With that stare emblazoned in my memory, the bobcat bounded away, off through the sagebrush and never to be seen again. But it was the last time I did laundry at the field station without bringing my binoculars. Just in case.

I liked to think about the coyotes, badger, and bobcat as I sat out on the porch of Owl West each evening, gingerly holding my bowl of micro-waved Progresso soup. A sixty-mile round trip to the nearest grocery and no personal vehicle made for little excitement in the culinary department, but kind care packages from a couple of Silverton birders and the wildlife made up for it. As I slurped my soup, kingbirds sailed across the station, meadowlarks poured melodies from rabbitbrush like shots of honey, and swallows dipped and dove for mosquitoes. Meanwhile, I tried to avoid spooning mosquitoes into my soup, long since resigned to their exploitation of my arms and legs. I listened to the desert revving up for night and waited for that golden sliding light of 8 o'clock. When it came, I knew it was time to lace up my sneakers and take my sunset run. The colors were a little different each of those fifty-five summer sunsets, but their patterns started to feel like home to me. I was almost becoming a part of the place.

This growing sense of belonging was bittersweet. I would be leaving soon, and Malheur seemed to know it. As the long days of summer wore down on their edges, the refuge began to feel restless. It, too, was moving on from summer. Flocks of migrant shorebirds descended upon the marshes, their tundra-born cries blowing across the mudflats. Each day, more dowitchers and yellowlegs arrived, soon outnumbering the ducks on our surveys. Yellowthroats ceased their ratcheting songs, preparing to lift from their cattail haunts and venture south for winter. Shrikes appeared again at the field station, teaching their young to swoop down on grasshoppers from the station power lines.

On our last week of butterfly surveys, a tattered pair of ghostly white wings drifted among the milkweed: a monarch at the end of its life, its orange scales lost to the wear of time. Papery and translucent, this monarch will soon settle into the Malheur dust, leaving her children to complete the remarkable round-trip journey begun by her great-grandparents in southern California.

As the monarchs disappear, white-lined sphinx moths arrive in force, flashing black and white and pink among clusters of thistles across the refuge. Migrant rufous hummingbirds return to the headquarters feeders, and a stirring wind carries the *thrrrup*s of the first fall tanagers out to my boss's trailer from the headquarters cottonwoods. The members of Malheur's science staff are moving, too—first back into their old buildings, vacant since the uproar of the winter occupation, then away. North. West. Like me.

On August 7th at sundown, I ran up the butte for the last time. At the top I stood, staring quietly eastward at the soft deep rainbow of light that rises invisibly behind most watchers of sunsets. As our star sank farther beneath the westward horizon, a deep blue line—the earth's shadow—climbed up from the Steens. Coyotes rallied in a high wailing chorus, surrounding me briefly in sound and then vanishing into silence. Dust and sage and the scent of rain filled my nostrils. A storm was mounting in the north, clouds pillowing and darkening in the gleam of the first planets.

I stayed up on the butte all that night, feeling the raindrops splattering, smattering, soaking life into the soil around me and smelling the reawakening of change in the desert. Stars silvered the edges of a great storm-cloud as it roiled above me. Evocations of unseen nighthawks floated down from the darkness.

I knew then that although I'd be leaving the next day, a part of me would be left here: a breathlessness, a quiet, a listening, a wonder. Something infinite. And I knew that I would have to keep coming back to find it again.

I breathed in and smiled into the night.

URSULA K. LE GUIN

Artemisia tridentata

Some ruthlessness befits old age.
Tender young herbs are generous and pliant,
but in dry solitude the grey-leaved sage
stands unforthcoming and defiant.

No bird is so iconic of daily experience at the Malheur Field Station and other human establishments in the basin as the comical, tolerant, and uniquely graceful common nighthawk. Trawling the skies for insects or perched on a fence railing, from June through early September these are the summer neighbors all visitors and residents get to know. Here we get a hands-on look at these famous and friendly birds.

HARRY FULLER

The Nighthawks of Malheur

Malheur is home to a bird whose way of living is astonishing but its American name is nonsense. It is called the "common nighthawk." In summary, it is not common, not a night bird, not a hawk. When I first came to admire this bird, my birding group was staying at the Malheur Field Station. I was leading a June birding field trip. One morning a staff member there mist-netted a local bird. This person held the nighthawk with its belly exposed as our group stood in a close flock, staring at the bird. It was the first time any of us birders had been two feet from a common nighthawk. This bird was held gently with one finger on either side of its head, a thumb lightly across its breast. At nine inches, this dark bird was only slightly longer than the person's hand. Its wings tapered to a sharp point, and they extended beyond the tip of the tail. When a wing was opened gently, it revealed how this small bird could have a wingspan of up to two feet. Each wing had a single, bright, white bar on the otherwise dark, mottled plumage. The captive's two large, dark eyes watched us.

We could not know if the bird felt fear, anger, or hatred. It occasionally protested its captivity with a hissing sound, reptilian in tone.

The staffer gently opened the bird's two-inch-wide mouth and we watchers all gasped in surprise. We were looking at a tiny sieve: several insects were caught on the bristles inside the cotton-white mouth. There the insects stick until the bird swallows to make room for the next catch. I could envision the long wings, the cruising speed of twenty miles per hour, the wide mouth for catching flying insects. How is the nighthawk so successful a hunter? Over short distances it outraces the insects. A mosquito travels at about 1.5 miles per hour; the nighthawk can move more than ten times as fast. A common nighthawk wings across the sky with its mouth wide open and overtakes flying insects, sweeping up its next meal. Its prey includes almost all insects you can find aloft in any particular habitat. A single nighthawk stomach was once found to contain five hundred mosquitoes. They also devour mayflies, beetles, caddisflies, flying ants, moths, wasps, and grasshoppers.

Admiring the nighthawk's large mouth, we almost ignored its tiny beak. It had to be carefully pointed out to us. The bill is inconspicuous, nestled among stiff little feathers lining the bird's mouth. A nighthawk feeds without ever using this irrelevant beak. The mouth is two inches wide with the tiny bill right in the center. The bill is hardly more than ceremonial, good for preening and nothing else. But the small beak was not the bird's most surprising preening tool, as we soon found out.

Before the bird was released to go back to its daytime siesta, we were shown its two spindly little legs and equally fragile-looking toes and talons. We were all surprised after seeing the feet of blackbirds, sparrows, woodpeckers, warblers, quail. Each of these birds can walk, run, or hop. Each can jump or grip a limb. Some even rake the ground to find food. Many songbirds, including the robin, can clamp down on a limb to perch and then lock that grip by cocking their ankle. That way they do not fall as they sleep while perched. It takes a deliberate move on the part of a perched songbird to release that locked grip. The nighthawk's feet are not fit for limb-grabbing or prey-crushing. There is no grasping strength in those tiny toes. The bird cannot perch by clutching a limb. If it lands on a level or gently curved surface, it can balance there. At rest the nighthawk lies on its belly. Its tiny legs tuck up inside the feathers. It may rest at night on the ground or in a road, or land in a tree where it lines up parallel with the limb. It can also lie on fence rails, stumps, rooftops, and other smooth surfaces. On the ground the nighthawk has been known to walk or scuttle only short distances. Our group talked about all this before we faced our next surprise: a single toe on one foot is equipped with a row of fine teeth perpendicular to the toe's length. This is a built-in comb used to clean the feathers around the bird's mouth. You gotta keep the food delivery area clean.

While it is fascinating to see the unusual physiognomy of the nighthawk at close range, so is watching their performance aloft. Their aerial elegance against a sunny blue sky is mesmerizing. Now I often time my Malheur visits to coincide with the spring arrival of the common nighthawks. Their season on these northerly breeding grounds is short. They are usually the last migrant breeding species to return each spring. The year's first nighthawks at Malheur are usually seen in late May with the bulk of the population arriving by June 10th. The nighthawk numbers begin to dwindle in late summer, falling sharply in September. There are no sightings of this species after mid-October until the next May.

Common nighthawks generally feed at dawn and dusk. On sufficiently warm nights you may see and hear them hawking moths near bright lights at the field station or in Frenchglen. The bonus to an early June visit is that, right after their spring return, nighthawks are sufficiently hungry to hunt any time of day. At that time you have the best chance to spot dozens feeding in midday, under bright skies in full sunlight. Bring your camera. You can sometimes watch nighthawks swarming through the air over Benson Pond or the field station. We are used to smaller swallows or even black terns aloft, but these long-winged birds make a bolder spectacle. The flight of feeding or courting nighthawks is good reason to stand in an open spot at Malheur, your binoculars to your eyes and your mouth agape in wonder, and observe these aerialists at their daily work. Their flight has variously been described as bouncy, bouyant, jerky, moth-like. Pete Dunne puts it this way: "A wheeling, drunken-looking, falcon-like bird feeding high overhead at dawn and dusk."

There is a moment watching nighthawks in flight when I suddenly wish to be one, if only for an hour. One often circles or turns tightly two or three hundred feet above our earth. The bird may be calling out from overhead, then at the end of an arc it starts a shallow dive. The goddess

gravity enhances its speed and a watcher can imagine that effortless accel-
eration, the thrill of free energy granted by the earth herself. You can
understand why I envy the nighthawk and its relationship with air and
the physics of flight.

During a June visit to Malheur you can see the courtship activities of
the common nighthawk. It is one of the many species that uses particular
flight behavior as part of the annual courtship ritual. The male makes his
vertical plunge to attract a mate. The females will not nest in marshy areas;
they require dry ground around the nest site, and at Malheur, the female
settles onto some small open area out among the sagebrush. The male tar-
gets his demonstrative dive, which may begin as high as a hundred feet (far
higher than the similar vertical plunge of the male Anna's hummingbird),
to be directly over her head. He shoots downward at about a seventy-de-
gree angle and can break off the dive less than ten feet above the ground.
I hold my breath until I see him pull up at the end of each potentially
suicidal drop. Whew. The percussion of the nighthawk's boom, caused
by violent vibration of the wing feathers as the bird brakes its plunge,
makes it unique among bird sounds at Malheur. It is. Some observers
have referred to the sound as a thunderclap. This courtship booming is
a flamboyant display of nighthawk uniqueness. In wide-open spots you
may see male nighthawks make their aerial proposals—overlooking the
basin below Krumbo Lake, the parking lot at the visitor's center, Central
Patrol Road where you have an open view south of the field station.

When courtship is consummated, the female lays her pair of eggs in
a small, open area. Occasionally she will nest atop a rock or stump, usually only a few feet above the ground. Each small egg is cream or olive
colored with splotches of gray or brown. No nest building, no carrying
of moss or sticks, no mud nor saliva needed. The birds seem to depend
on camouflage for defense, making little effort to hide a nest site. They
do not even resort to killdeer-like pretense to lure aware possible predators. At Malheur each pair nests once per summer, and they lay only
two eggs. Nesting takes place in Malheur Basin's dry habitat, and the
sagebrush and other dense shrubs afford good protection from midday
sun and heat. Their main protection is lack of detection. As you can readily calculate, this is not a formula for a rapid population increase among
nighthawks.

Henry David Thoreau observed a nighthawk nest near his home in Concord back in 1853: "Visited my nighthawk on her nest. Could hardly believe my eyes when I stood within seven feet and beheld her sitting on her eggs, her head to me. She looked so Saturnian, so one with the earth, so sphinxlike. . . . It was not an actual living creature, far less a winged creature of the air, but a figure in stone or bronze, a fanciful production of art."

Ornithologist George M. Sutton spent considerable time around nighthawks during his career in Oklahoma. He particularly liked studying and drawing young birds and had this to say about nighthawk hatchlings: "The chicks are delightful. When very young they pay little attention to those who stand over them; but when they become sparrow-size and their wing quills are feathering out, they have a most amusing way of opening their big mouths and hissing while at the same time spreading wide those utterly useless wings and running slowly off in a straight line like an ancient galleon under full sail."

Generally the female is around the young and the male feeds his mate and young by regurgitation. Feeding of the young happens during the hunting periods of dawn and dusk. By early August at Malheur you can watch young nighthawks in the air, feeding with the adults. Nighthawk feeding areas are often above marsh, irrigated fields, or open water as the insect numbers there are often greater. From one night to the next the feeding flocks are unpredictable as they must follow the winds and the insect hordes as conditions change through the summer. I tend to see nighthawks feeding higher in the air than swallows or black terns.

By late June the nighthawks have begun nesting and they've settled into their morning and evening feeding routine. Their morning flights begin about an hour before actual sunrise and end a quarter hour or so after the sunrise. Evening flights begin about a half hour before sunset and run an hour or more afterwards. At both ends of the day their feeding times lean toward less light. While they feed you will hear the nighthawks' call, a loud, nasally "peent." Inside the field station dorms the sound comes through even closed windows. It can be heard inside an RV or a tent at Page Springs. The call has a quality and sound that cannot be confused with any other sound at Malheur. The nighthawks' call is most obvious when the birds are in flight. Because they fly with their mouths open most of the time, we groundlings cannot tell if they make the sound deep in their throat or only when the mouth is ajar. They also make calls from nesting or roosting areas while on the ground. Sometimes you may hear the familiar call and look up, seeing no bird in the air.

The nighthawk's very specific diet and feeding methods limit their flexibility. They can only feed on flying insects. For nighthawks to get enough to eat, the insect population must be sufficient and the weather warm enough to have those flying insects in the air. The nighthawk's specialized mouth lets it drink water from streams and lakes as it skims across the surface. Nighthawks thrive at Malheur where insects are plentiful and there is always open water where they can drink.

There is only one other nightjar species breeding at Malheur. It is the smaller, lighter-colored common poorwill. Poorwills do not hunt from flight like the larger nighthawks. Poorwills lie along roads and other open areas while hunting after dark. This bird watches for an individual moth or other flying insect and then launches itself from the ground for the attack. After the dusk feeding period when it's truly dark, male nighthawks also often roost along gravel roads. Both species are frequent road-kill as a result. Either species may appear in your headlights if you are driving the back roads after dark. In front of a vehicle the paler poorwill appears almost ghostly while the nighthawk looks like a dark shadow and the white wing bars often flash in the headlights.

When common nighthawks begin to migrate south in late summer, they face thousands of miles of travel. Most Malheur nighthawks will winter east of the Andes from Ecuador and Brazil southward. That could be as far as seven thousand miles one way even if the migration path is fairly direct. Common nighthawks make one of the longest annual migrations of any bird breeding in North America. When nighthawks migrate they can fly both day and night.

For good viewing of nighthawks at rest I suggest hunting through the scattered groves of large trees in the Malheur Basin. In the sagebrush they can be almost impossible to find. Check the large willows at the north end of Benson Pond. Try the cottonwoods and fence railings at the visitor's center. Check the Russian olives and wooden fences at the field station. There the birds have become habituated to people and you are just like the passing breeze, no concern. One June we had a nighthawk regularly sleeping on the porch railing of our dorm as we came and went. Many times I have walked around the field station campus and counted sleeping nighthawks. Three in that Russian olive, one on the wooden fence outside our dorm, one on a porch railing, another on the fence of the children's playground, one on a flat roof, two more in yet another Russian olive, one on a fence post, one on top of a utility wire, another on top of a street lamp. Field station staff have counted up to fifty individual nighthawks roosting there at one time. With a little practice you, too, can quickly get used to spotting that dark, arched lump on a horizontal surface. Large head on one end, dark plumage that nearly disappears in deep shade, a tapered body that stretches backward to the pointed ends of those long wings.

If the bird is down low, you may approach within a few yards. Sometimes one is less than three feet off the ground. Get your sleeping nighthawk pictures, stare at and be stared at, even sit down and wait to see what happens. This species has long been known for its relative tameness around people and its lack of wariness. I often think we people must be so big and slow, compared to what matters in the nighthawk's world of flight and small insects, that we seem harmless or irrelevant. When the bird does decide to take off, the first flap lifts the bird off its resting spot and it is airborne. It rises at a steep angle as its long wings quickly build up air speed.

The Malheur Basin population must number in the many thousands, if not greater. In many other areas this bird is now scarce where it was once abundant. In sections of the United States, nighthawks have become uncommon owing to the usual factors: pesticides and loss of nesting habitat. They even did fine for decades in cities when tar and gravel roofs afforded nesting places. Now plastic roofs are too slick and turn them away. From 1966 through 2014 it is estimated the US population of common nighthawk fell by 61 percent. The 2014 State of the Birds Report listed this species as being in steep decline. We can hope the Malheur population will continue to be protected and thus successful. If so, you and I and many future generations of wildlife admirers can meet and learn to admire this spectacular creature who lives in a way most of animals could not.

*As if watched by Bendire's ghost, German transplant Hendrik Herlyn
came to Malheur as a young birder. Then he somehow persuaded his parents to come visit from Germany not once but twice and showed them
the waters and the mountain. Steens Mountain became their iconic
memory of eastern Oregon. Hendrik takes us along.*

HENDRIK HERLYN

The German Visitors, Part 2

In March of 1989, another native of Germany paid his first visit to the
area south of the erstwhile Camp Harney visited by Charles Bendire, better known today as Malheur National Wildlife Refuge. I had arrived in
Oregon in the summer of 1988 as an exchange student from Germany to
pursue my master's degree in wildlife science at Oregon State University
in Corvallis (little did I know at the time that I would permanently settle
in this town). An avid birder since my early teenage years, I was intrigued
by the reports I heard about a magical place called Malheur National
Wildlife Refuge, somewhere in the far southeastern corner of the state.
So, during spring break of 1989, I jumped into my newly acquired VW
microbus and headed east over the mountains to explore this part of Oregon, which at the time was still entirely unknown to me.

Having traversed the late-winter landscape of Klamath and Lake
Counties, I finally arrived at Malheur refuge, where I found myself
utterly awed by the sheer magnitude of open space. I marveled at the
vast expanse of sagebrush country and the seemingly endless marshland,
edged by towering rimrock and dominated to the southeast by the maj-

esty of snow-covered Steens Mountain. I watched small herds of mule deer feed along the willow-lined Donner und Blitzen River and smiled at the sight of fleet-footed pronghorn prancing through the sagebrush steppes. At one point, my heart almost stopped when a badger suddenly waddled across the road in front of me, and at night, huddled in my down bag in the back of my camper van, I was serenaded to sleep by the eerie laughter of a pack of coyotes.

And of course, there were birds—birds everywhere you looked! Although it was still early in the year and spring migration—one of the main magnets that draws birders from all over the state and elsewhere to this remote wilderness in late May and early June—had not yet started in earnest, the air was filled with the amazing spectacle of thousands of snow and Ross's geese taking wing, joined by flocks of Canada geese and countless species of ducks. For the first time, I heard the drawn-out bugle call of the sandhill cranes—a sound so full of longing and promise that it touched me at my very core and from that moment on became indelibly linked to the vast beauty of this big-sky country. The marshes rang with the song of red-winged blackbirds, long-billed curlews were already displaying over the meadows, and great horned owls eyed me suspiciously from their cottonwood perches at refuge headquarters.

I was hooked, and when I finally pointed my van north and west again, I knew I would be coming back soon.

This first visit to Malheur National Wildlife Refuge was the beginning of a lifelong love affair with a place whose beauty is rivaled by few others I've encountered in my travels around much the world. As for many other Oregon birders, the refuge would soon become the destination of an annual pilgrimage for me during the height of spring migration, both to enjoy the beauty of the diverse countryside and its many feathered denizens and also to look for rare vagrants, one of the special allures in this desert country dotted by lush oases of tall cottonwoods, which serve as magnets for unusual warblers, vireos, flycatchers, and other songbirds from the eastern United States that get blown of course during their migration. In most years I return again in the fall, when birds move through on their way south, and the countryside has taken on an entirely different, yet equally alluring aspect. Plus, in late summer and fall, it is finally possible to ascend all the way to the top of Steens Mountain, where you can enjoy the breathtaking vistas across Kiger Gorge and the wide expanse of the Alvord Desert below, and, with luck, come across a flock of black rosy-finches along the edge of a snow field.

Over the years, I have traveled to Malheur more times than I can remember, occasionally by myself, but more often in the company of one or several of my many friends and birding companions. Yet, of all the trips, two stand out as particularly memorable, since I was fortunate enough to introduce my parents to this magical place when they first came to visit me in the summer of 1990, and to take them back there another time, in the fall of 2002. Both of my parents fell in love with Malheur, and especially with Steens Mountain—in fact, during their second (and final) visit, a repeat trip up the Steens was the number one item on their itinerary! Their firsthand experience with this amazing corner of Oregon, perhaps more than any other part of the state, made them understand a little bet-

Habbo Herlyn, Hendrik Herlyn, and Alan Contreras at the Malheur Field Station, 2002. Photo by Elisabeth Herlyn.

ter why their eldest son had chosen to build a life so far away from home.

As a birder herself, my mom was right in her element as I pointed out the various species in the desert, marshes, willows and mountains, while my dad leaned back, smoking his ever-present pipe, and enjoyed the vast landscapes, their geology and history. But both of my folks enjoyed some of the birding highlights—the pairs of bugling sandhill cranes in the marshes; the cuteness of a family of burrowing owls, staring at us from a small mound among the sagebrush; a bright hooded warbler, an awesome bird's-eye view of an ovenbird in one of the lilac hedges and a sleepy-eyed flammulated owl perched near the parking lot, all at the refuge headquarters; the haunting song and striking plumage of the western meadowlarks; a flock of more than a hundred black rosy-finches against the backdrop of the Alvord Desert; and the ever-present great horned owls at headquarters and Benson Pond. They particularly enjoyed a fearless porcupine as it lumbered right through our campsite at Page Springs, where we fell asleep to the call of a poorwill and woke in the morning to the spiraling song of a canyon wren.

I will forever treasure my memories of these visits, which I know left a lasting expression on my parents—they frequently talked about their time at Malheur and the Steens when we saw each other or spoke on the phone.

There is one other trip to Malheur National Wildlife Refuge that deserves special mention: In September 2013, my husband Oscar and I traveled there to spend our honeymoon together. Although we had shared twenty years as a couple already, it was only in 2013 that the laws finally changed and we were able to get legally married. We celebrated this wonderful and long overdue event by embarking on a camping trip to this beautiful corner of Oregon. We've been back every spring and fall since and hope to continue this tradition for many years to come.

Fast forward to the epilogue, page 179, to conclude this story.

ALAN L. CONTRERAS

Malheur at 14

He brought me here
when I was fourteen,
my hair long and dark much as yours is,
and I brought your mother
before she was ten
to see the great marsh and the mountain.

We stopped over there
by the cottonwood tree,
it was one of six then newly planted,
and the oriole's nest
—see it there, hanging down?—
was farther west by the old fountain.

This is the place,
he told me back then
where my ashes will join with the curlews
and where year after year
I can be there in May
when the cranes dance over the meadows.

So I brought you today
to show you the place
that he thought was closest to heaven
in the hope that someday
you'll think of me here
by the waters below the great mountain.

Most of us think of Malheur and the Steens Mountain region as a place to visit. Yet it is also a place to work. That work is more than serving the high-season needs of tourists or hunters—several thousand people live in the high desert of southeastern Oregon. The work they do can be outside the experience of an average tourist, as Chas Biederman relates in his story of learning a new job on the mountain.

CHAS BIEDERMAN

Packing with WZ

In 2006, the BLM awarded Warren Matthews,[1] the owner of Harney County Mule Company, a contract to pack fence and wire out of the Steens wildérness. I was twenty-one at the time and enjoyed working with Warren and his mules. So when I heard about the opportunity to join him, I jumped on it. Warren always figured out how to have fun even if we were riding green mules and getting thrown off every day. And the Steens had been a place that I felt an affinity toward since the first time I visited the mountain in 2003. We had seven miles' worth of material we ended up packing out that summer, and it turned out to be one of the hardest jobs I've ever had.

Warren spent days figuring out different methods of packing the fencing material and finally settled on welding bent rebar to form racks that could be attached to each side of a mule. These racks allowed posts to rest horizontally and provided a basket for the wire. In order to protect the mules, Warren cut out carpet that he draped over the decker pack saddles so that the mules would not be chafed by the wire and posts. Loaded, the packed mules looked like they had rockets attached to both sides as the posts stuck out almost past their necks. Without much work, these posts could poke another mule or ram someone standing on the ground or in the saddle. The racks could also get stuck together if one mule went out of place and got too close to another mule's set of racks. But all of these hazards didn't discourage Warren from setting off into the Steens with nine green-broke mules that had never been packed before.

It is best to understand Warren as an optimist. Warren saw the contract as a great opportunity to train mules and spend the summer in the Steens. If he hadn't won the contract, he would have still trained mules that summer, and he knew that the best way to train a mule would be to give it a job that it had to work every day. He had the same approach with the delinquent boys that came to live in his house. Both mules and boys learned a lot from working from Warren.

When I say that the mules were green, I mean they weren't even used to being tied up and led around by the halter yet. Just getting the mules to follow each other down the trail was a challenge. They would see a rock and imagine a bear. To protect themselves, the mules would move way off the trail, pulling the rest of the string with them. This would be the perfect recipe for a wreck. Luckily Warren had the common sense to not hook them all together. Instead we had three strings of three mules.

Two other boys, Stewart and River, my dad, and my kid brother, Drew, who was twelve at the time, helped Warren pack that first day. We started out before sunrise. And we had to. Getting the green mules brushed up, saddled, and attached to racks required extreme diligence and patience. The mules didn't like it when we were along their sides. They didn't like the saddle pads or the saddles or, for that matter, much of anything else we did around them.

To get the cinch under their bellies, we had to have someone pass it from the other side to avoid getting kicked in the head. The britchens made them suck up their butts. But the racks were the worst of all. Some of the mules needed us to distract them by covering their eyes or twisting an ear or both to get the rebar near their sides. After attached, the mules often pranced around scaring themselves, their neighbors, and the riding mules with the heavy rattling of the racks.

We started packing the mules the same way we saddled them—by hobbling a leg. Once we felt they were fairly well situated, we would slowly set the posts on the racks, making as little noise as possible. The mules were not used to having long objects project along their sides. They would get scared and move one way or another, making whoever was along their side dance to avoid being run over or jarred. Other mules would stand, not bothered by the sight of the posts but not used to carrying the weight. They would bow lower and lower as we added posts. They were winding themselves up for a fantastic blow. And then, once they couldn't get any lower, they would jump, and the racks would bang without mercy against their sides, causing the mules to buck.

Once a mule started bucking, it had enough energy to throw the posts off its racks, lightening the load and encouraging the mule to keep up the rhythmic momentum to lose as much foreign weight as possible. These nine mules threw posts with passion and fury. Grunting, wailing, twisting, and kicking, they would not stop until maybe only a single post would be dangling from a side. Then we would try again. We would slowly place the t-posts on the racks and prepare for the mule to blow again. Some of them threw off their loads three or four times that day and only after being completely drenched by sweat would they finally accept the weight.

This work did not bring us joy but we laughed endlessly to keep things bearable. We spent most of the time laughing at each other and the mistakes only Warren was able to avoid. We fumbled with the fencing pliers and wire. The straps kept needing to be adjusted because they were not put on correctly when we first saddled. By the time it was two in the afternoon, all of us were out of water and exhausted.

We had to send my brother to refill our bottles. None of us had been up in this part of the Steens before, but Drew felt confident that he could find his way to the last creek crossing and back. He was gone for over two hours, and, as the minutes ticked by, my Dad grew concerned. We had to convince my dad that my brother was okay, which was difficult to do at this point because nothing about the day was working out very well.

When we finally got our loads together it was seven or eight with the evening approaching. My brother finally showed up bearing full water bottles, relieving my dad's concern. Now he had to manage a pack mule behind him, as we decided to separate the strings even farther so that my dad, River, Warren, and myself would be leading pack mules.

Any relief in having my brother back was quickly brushed from my father's consciousness as one of the mules behind my dad fell to the ground. The mule began kicking his stomach like he had colic.

"What should we do?" my dad asked as we stared in disbelief.

"I guess we'll have to unload him. Something's not right," Warren replied. Something was definitely not right.

We got off our mules and separated our strings. None of the mules seemed nearly as tired as me. They were still on edge, which made me very attentive in breaking the pig ties that kept my string together. The sick mule was now just lying there not attempting to move. Instead it was swatting its tail and groaning. The posts clanged as we took them off his back. All the other mules would have taken this opportunity to demonstrate their athletic ability with us making noise like that, but this mule didn't move. It was clearly sick. All we could do was unload the mule and hope that he would follow us back to camp. The mule never did. Instead he stood up with a wobble and awkwardly trotted into the juniper. Years later, we would find out he was picked up by a couple of hunters and sold to another party.

It was very dark now, and the Ankle Creek Trail, which wasn't familiar to any of us in the daylight, now seemed like riding on a distant continent. Once moving, any packer knows that it is better not to stop unless you have to. Stopping will encourage the mules to get into trouble. Warren headed off ahead of us as he was riding a fast walking mule named Zodiac, and my brother went with him; that left the rest of us to follow out of sight of his string. We didn't realize exactly how far ahead he was until one of his pack mules came running back toward us.

My brother and Warren had stopped at Mud Creek, which is a creek crossing you come to after traversing the drainage's side hill. Those few moments waiting gave one of the mules an opportunity to poke another, scaring it free from the pack string. The liberated mule got it in his head that one of us riders behind him was going to be able to fix all these problems with the racks and the steel posts, and he was right. He ran straight back up the hill toward the rest of the party and made sparks fly as the posts he was now dragging slammed against the rocks in the trail.

We could hear the mule coming a few moments before we could see the sparks and only when the beast was within thirty feet of us could we view who he was.

It turned out to be Stumpy—a squatty-looking mule with a name easy to remember. This mule was never going to make a high-dollar riding mule, but, that night, Stumpy got all of our attention. The rest of the mules were also very much aware. I tried to get my mules off the trail, but they wouldn't budge. They had their ears cocked and were listening for the danger Stumpy must be running from. By the time he was in view, the other mules were ready to start a stampede. After some impressive jumps, twists, and pulls, we now had an elaborate crescendo of dancing mules all skilled in losing t-posts. They scattered in every direction like charged electrons. The clanging didn't stop for several moments, but riding in the dust of chaos, I focused entirely on my riding mule. She decided to take the higher ground behind us and mix with the juniper, making me tuck down close so that I would not get brushed off by one of the many branches.

My dad's riding mule and one of the other pack mules—Little Rose— chose a different direction, heading straight down the hill vertically from the trail. Luckily my dad was able to get ahold of his mule's head and turned it back to the trail, but Little Rose didn't stop until she was at the bottom. We had not brought flashlights that day. Night riding wasn't on the schedule. So when the mules scattered, we could hear where they went but not see where they were. We could hear Little Rose down at the bottom of the drainage wrestling a fallen juniper with her racks. I had been on this trail only the morning before, so I did not know exactly how far below me the mule was. But I knew that the mule needed help. Little Rose was a small red roan with a star on her forehead. She turned into a great pack mule that trip, but on the first day out, she was inexperienced and riled up like the rest of them.

"Chas, I wouldn't go down there," Stewart exclaimed.

"Stewart, he's already down there!" my father replied.

All of this was foreign to us. The location, the packing, the mules—at this point no one knew what to do. Only Warren had experience packing. The rest of us were as green as the mules. It took me awhile to get down to her, having to crawl over fallen juniper and sagebrush. And when I got to her, it was so dark that I couldn't tell which side was her tail or her head. She was just a black blob covered by a willow bush and pinned down by a fallen juniper. That night, I learned a lot about Little Rose's disposition. She let me feel around her body as she lay still among the dark shadows. The first thing I figured out was her tail. As my eyes adjusted, I could tell she had tipped her load and the saddle was pulled to one side with the britchen and breast collar twisted close to her body. I relieved the cinch. Little Rose took a heavy breath out but the breast collar and britchen were so tightly wrapped around her that I couldn't just unbuckle them. I had to get her to stand up first and that meant undoing the racks that were pinning her against the log.

River came down not long after I released the cinch. We decided that we would ease Little Rose up with the halter and see if she could get herself unstuck. River pulled on the halter, and I pushed her butt. I told River he better find a place to go if she did get up and decided to move forward. He stomped down some willow branches and said he was fine. "Just keep pushing." She began to get up but got caught by the racks, which forced her to lay down again. She was still stuck. But now her head was up so at least I could now see the straps holding the saddle against her body. I put a knife between her and the breast collar. The leather tore easily against the sharp blade. The racks still loaded with t-posts rattled a little. Now we could try to push the racks over her back. She was free of the saddle and no longer stuck to the log, so we encouraged her to stand but she wouldn't budge. She decided she was safer lying on the ground.

None of the other mules had gotten pinned down like Little Rose. Some of them were still dragging posts, others lost their posts and had both racks flipped to one side or had the saddle pulled under their bellies, but they were all standing. By the time we caught up with all the mules and freed them of their loads, it was past midnight. We finally met up with Warren, who told us what had happened down at Mud Creek with Stumpy and would later laugh about how he and my brother also struggled to relieve the loads with only the glow of his watch to provide light.

We left Little Rose in the drainage that night and the rest of the string except one at the bottom of the hill along the trail tied up with their saddles next to them. The only mule we brought back somehow lost its racks but still had its saddle on. It was dark enough that we couldn't really see the trail. We had to rely on our saddle mule to lead us to camp. I was following all the other riders, and, by this time, my riding mule was fed up with being poked in the butt by the pack mules and their t-posts. She found an opportunity to tell me how she felt about the situation when a tree branch snapped back at her ears. No one saw the rodeo, but even if it had been light out there wouldn't have been much time to watch the entertainment. She was done with me in an instant, catapulting me head-first into a pile of rocks.

One thing I can tell you about the Steens is that it is made up of a whole lot of rocks. So being in a pile of them wasn't that shocking. What was shocking was that I could see stars above me even though I was looking at the ground. Those stars faded as I stood up and wiped my brow. Ebony—my riding mule—was standing a few feet away waiting for another opportunity to remind me again how pissed off she was. Now every branch that moved was an excuse for her to jerk one way or another, and I had to keep the reins ready to prevent her from losing it again. Warren and River began calling her Helen Keller—the mule that couldn't see—and I spent the rest of the night cursing them and then my mule.

The Ankle Creek Trail at that time was grown over at a section that runs along Mud Creek, so following the trail in the dark was next to impossible. Warren said he was going to let the reins go on his riding mule and that she would find the way back. But Zodiac, Warren's mule, ended up doing a big circle around a willow bush and headed back toward the rest of us. This wasn't too reassuring for a party now completely defeated and exhausted, but that was just how things happened with Warren and his mules. Warren lined Zodiac up again the way we needed to go before she took a detour around the willow bush, and this time she led us back on the trail.

The trail felt like it went on forever that night. And before we were back at camp, the one pack mule Warren was ponying summarized our experience that day by rolling her saddle under her belly. She pulled hard against the lead rope Warren was holding. I got off Helen Keller and relieved the cinch and breast collar from the pack mule. The pack saddle fell to the ground. "Just leave it," Warren told me. That's right. That night when we got back to camp we brought back only one pack mule with no posts, wire, or even a pack saddle.

The next morning, I felt like I had been run over by a cement truck—twice. I wasn't even out of my sleeping bag yet. We had to change our strategy. We had to get better at how we packed our loads. Maybe today we wouldn't try to pack nine—maybe just three. When we got back to the mules, we could see they were fresh and ready to teach some more lessons about what it means to be green. After making sure they had plenty to drink, we saddled them and ponied three up the trail to collect some of the scattered posts. We got better that day, but still it took us till nine o'clock at night to come back with the three loads. The day after we came back with six, and this time with daylight. By the end of the summer, we were dialed in and having fun, but that first day up on the Steens showed us how tough packing can be.

Note

1   WZ is the livestock brand used by Warren Matthews.

There are many ways to experience the refuge, the desert, and the moun-tain. Each offers the pleasures and challenges of seasonal change as well as a change in what we see. Sometimes an individual experiences the mountain in very different ways. Sean Burns was a high school distance runner who remains actively interested in the birds of the mountain. We get to see both sides of his experience here.

SEAN BURNS

Two Sides of the Mountain

Mountains are often regarded as sacred places, and Steens Mountain feels no different. Beneath the whisper of the aspen I can almost hear a heartbeat, the rhythm of the mountain. Perhaps this is what draws me to the monolith of basalt rock; perhaps it is the feeling of seclusion that the slopes of the mountain bring. Whatever the cause, it attracts me and many others from across the country.

I first came to the mountain as an athlete. For one week each sum-mer, approximately two hundred high-school runners, including myself, reside on the slopes of Steens Mountain. The name of this event is Steens Mountain High Elevation Running Camp. The purpose of the camp is to train our body, the mind, and connect with nature. Technology is shunned. There is no music, no phones, no outside disturbances, only the sound of the birds and the wind in the trees.

Steens Mountain High Elevation Running Camp is not for the faint of heart. I lived in accommodations that amounted to a set of twenty person canvas tents bought as surplus from the US Army and whatever sleeping pads and bags we brought with ourselves. Sanitary facilities at the camp were limited to fifteen portable toilets and a couple sets of hand-washing stations. The one item not lacking at the camp was food. Even so, most campers, myself included, lost two to four pounds over the course of the week due to the altitude, which was over seven thousand feet, and the work performed.

The first day of camp starts with, unsurprisingly, running. At this point even small amounts of exertion, such as running up a small hill, made my lungs start crying for oxygen. The day was mixed with short runs and sessions of yoga to acclimate all of our bodies to the altitude. When compared to the rest of the week, it was exceedingly easy.

On the second day of camp, we all boarded the four rented school buses at six o'clock in the morning and drove almost to the top of the mountain, to the top of Big Indian Gorge. There, everyone disembarked and were told to start hiking. It was a single-file line on the narrow path down into the gorge. Everyone, all two hundred people, were silent, with the exception of the warning cry of "Rock!" when someone dislodged a large stone. The hike lasted a total of twenty-one miles to South Steens Campground. We were silent the whole time, enjoying our surroundings. The only noises were birds, the sound of footsteps, and the rushing of the creek flowing down the gorge. This part of the day passed quickly and was very enjoyable. The next fourteen miles were an extreme test of strength and endurance. It started with a seven-mile run up Little Blitzen Gorge to where the access trail enters at the head of the canyon.

Even while being pushed to the limit of my physical capabilities, I could not help but notice the sheer beauty of the area. By the time everyone was out of the canyon and headed back down the gravel road toward the camp, it was well past four o'clock. The mountain seemed to give strength to those who needed it, providing a breath of cooling wind or a grove of aspen to provide shade at the perfect moment. After the run, people claimed to have conquered the mountain, but really, the mountain let them win.

After a day of recovery, with minimal running, it was time for our next test: Cross Canyon. It was a three-mile race from Point A to Point B, with no trails, only a vague point toward the finish and GO! It crossed two small canyons, its namesake. During this race, we learned how to travel like mule deer bounding over bushes and rocks. We learned that some plants need to be avoided, such as the endemic Steens Mountain thistle, which has evolved a fearsome set of spines that not only scratch any exposed skin that brushed its leaves but also cause an unbearable itch. Plants such as the sagebrush and bitterbrush were dealt with by going over or through. The brush obtained minimal damage—the leg often yielded to the plant. The resulting scrapes and bruises were referred to as a "Steens Mountain Trail Map" almost affectionately. While at camp recovering from the race, we all gathered around the fire rings to compare battle scars.

The last two days of running camp were far more competitive, with small events that awarded each tent group points in the Steens Mountain Olympics. Events included the bar hang, where contestants dead hang from the bar for as long as possible; a relay race up the hilly, mile-long driveway to the main road; the bus pull, where teams pull a school bus on a rope for as far as possible; a cross-country style race up the main road; and the sagebrush sack hop. During the evening of the second to last day, there was a celebratory dinner that honors the Basque culture of the camp's founder and the sheepherders who were some of the first Europeans to live on the mountain. Camp tradition dictates that we had to find someone of the opposite gender and eat dinner with them. The next and final night of camp was the awards and recognitions ceremony. Awards were given out for such things as the winners of the Steens Mountain Olympics and the Cross Canyon race. Recognitions were also given out for multiyear campers: dog tags for three-year campers and Nike backpacks for four-year campers. The next morning, camp was closed with a run from the outskirts of the town of Burns to the high school, where the campers were dismissed on their way back home.

I came back to Steens Mountain for the birds. Researchers have long hypothesized that broad-tailed hummingbirds nest in the gorges of Steens Mountain, but it has never been confirmed. I decided to make my personal challenge to prove nesting of broad-tailed hummingbirds on the mountain.

I left home in mid-July with everything I would need for a week of camping on the mountain packed into the family's F150 pickup. I set up

my camp at the Fish Lake Campground, thirteen miles up the slope of
Steens, just a mile upslope from the site of where the running camp takes
place.

My first attempt to find the hummingbirds, on the evening of my
arrival, was at a small lake a few miles up the mountain from the campground. There were many of the closely related and much more common
rufous hummingbirds buzzing around. There was one female hummingbird that looked slightly different but after more thorough examination, I
concluded it was a rufous. After this attempt, I returned to my camp and
made dinner on a two-burner camp stove.

The first morning on the mountain, I decided to see if any male broad-
tailed hummingbirds were still up on the alpine "tundra," which is limited
to the summit ridge. This was also to be a scouting trip to identify other
places that may be suitable for the species. When I arrived on the tundra
later that morning, I found it to be very blustery and cold, which is not
suitable for high hummingbird activity. Regardless, I proceeded on up the
mountain where I observed a bright green blur blast in front of the truck,
seeming to exit the area directly above Big Indian Gorge. I can only draw
hypothetical conclusions as to the species of hummingbird, but the color,
size, and behavior of the bird lead to believe it was a male broad-tailed
hummingbird. Quickly parking the truck, I followed the hummingbird's
last-known trajectory toward the ridge where the mountain falls away. I
searched that section of the mountain for half an hour, until the icy wind
got the best of me and a mixture of graupel and snow began to fall.

The wind had intensified to the point where opening doors on the
windward side of the vehicle was out of the question. I drove up to the
summit parking lot, wondering what the mountain looked like in the
snow. As I sat there, the wind shaking the truck, a man walked out of
the snowstorm off the trail from Wildhorse Lake a mile down the hill.
It was his tracks, I assume, that another group followed up the mountain
when the trail became indistinguishable from the rest of the landscape.
After the bulk of the storm moved through, the temperatures dropped
significantly, so I suspended my efforts to find hummingbirds for the rest
of the day on the basis that activity would be limited at best. I returned
to camp and looked over the topographical maps of the mountain to plan
my next move.

The next day, I targeted a series of roads and ponds going farther up the mountain that looked like quality hummingbird habitat. This was after discovering that there was no effective way to enter the top of Big Indian Gorge and get back out short of hiking the twenty-one miles to South Steens Campground. This day's adventure turned out to be as fruitless as the first day's. There were a great many rufous hummingbirds in all plumages that made them all look different. After looking in what seemed to be every aspen grove, I called it a day and went back to camp. That night I decided to descend into Kiger Gorge following an old trail on its western wall the next day.

The following morning, I drove to the Kiger Gorge overlook and headed out toward the glacier-carved chasm. Everything was still cool and dewy at this point, and it made the quarter-mile hike to the trail a bit less enjoyable.

As soon as I dropped over the lip of the gorge, everything changed. The birds changed, the plants changed, the rocks were different, even the wind smelled different, more organic. It was like a new world. Almost immediately, I noticed the sound of running water, something absent from the main slope of the mountain. A family group of juncos were performing their best rosy-finch impression, waiting for insects to fly over the snowfield, get too cold to keep flying, and drop to the ice, where the birds fly in and feast. The farther I descended into the gorge, the more things changed. Willows grew on the banks of meltwater-fueled streams, and a family of Nashville warblers had settled and appeared to be thriving.

Hummingbirds were everywhere, feeding on the wildflowers that flourished all around, never pausing for more than a few seconds. Female rufous hummingbirds were numerous, and I observed the same mix of post-breeding raggedness that I had encountered before elsewhere on the mountain. About halfway down the wall of the gorge, what seemed to be a bit heavier-looking hummingbird flew behind a willow tree and perched out of view. I skirted the bush and the bird came into view. There before me was a female broad-tailed hummingbird in all of her subtle glory. Sitting in the hunched-over posture typical of her species, she displayed all the field marks clearly: buffy sides, neatly spotted cheeks, and wingtips that went only halfway down the tail. She flew out to an endemic Steens paintbrush flower and flared her tail, and I saw her orange outer tail feathers, paired with her green inner ones. It was an electrifying moment, confirming that the bird I was seeking was actually present.

After the broad-tailed hummingbird left the flower, I saw her a few more times in the area before continuing my descent. The bottom of the gorge was in sharp contrast to the rim. The cold, harsh, forbidding expanse was replaced with a warm, lush, diverse environment. The first male rufous hummingbird I found on that trip was at the bottom of Kiger Gorge. While hiking down the bottom of the canyon, a male Lazuli bunting perched not ten meters away and sang. The vibrant blues and rusts of his plumage stood out like a fine painting. Among the masses of female hummingbirds on the floor of the gorge, I managed to identify five more female broad-tailed hummingbirds buzzing around the aspen trees that lined the creek. At approximately 3 p.m., I headed back up the wall of the gorge. With the combination of altitude and incline making the ascent more strenuous, I took my time hiking up the wall. On the way back up, I noticed things that I did not on the way down, such as unique rock formations and plants such as orchids of the genus *Platanthera*.

An hour and a half into the hike to the rim, exhausted, I almost missed the seven greater sage-grouse that had moved into the area around the trailhead during the day. Though large birds, their camouflage matches the rocks almost exactly. Unfortunately, the one thing that I did not accomplish on this day was to prove breeding—all of the individuals I found were adult females.

The next morning, after making the drive down to Frenchglen to refuel, I followed an old side road down into a small canyon. Near the end of the road—and lacking any hummingbird sightings—I discovered the check engine light on the truck had illuminated. That effectively put an end to remote off-road explorations with the truck.

My last full day in the area I chose to spend birding on the Malheur National Wildlife Refuge. I saw fifty-one species of birds, including a rare marbled godwit. The experience of seeing the whole region up close, from where the life-giving water originates to where it ends up, brings the whole experience full circle. The next morning, I waved good-bye to the looming mountain of basalt rock that I had gotten in touch with the previous days. I hope it is not too long before I am honored to experience the mountain once again.

Life List

for Ash

After the news,
we drove the long day to the mountains,
taking water, some food, the tent
and a slim notebook into which
there wouldn't be time for writing. Instead,
a hike off the road on a muddy, elk-tracked path
Basque shepherds followed up Little Blitzen Creek.

The creek, rampant with runoff
turned us back into our own footsteps.

Sage and juniper filled the day like incense
in great churches, the smell at times
so strong it held us where we didn't know
we could stand silent for so long.

We were on the mountain but couldn't see it.
Fog and mist hardened to hail as we made our way
back to camp, our jackets freed of twigs
by the pelting.

At the Malheur Refuge, we counted this year's
migration: avocet, ibis, curlew, cinnamon teal,
swifts.

We remembered your list from the time we hiked
and you gave us brown creeper. Now ours
brims with white-faced ibis, sandhill crane.

They told us your brother's children
awoke at 3 a.m.
to a noisy bird at the window.

You release us to our flight-spray of moments—
then suddenly on the water, a flock.
We see a new bird and band it with memory.

Death is part of what we call life. Sometimes we feel it as a natural and necessary thing, part of the flow of time, the endless handing down of Earth to another generation. Sometimes it comes as a wave of unexpected ice and we recoil from the cold injustice of it. In the face of death, Quinton Hallett's preceding poem and Meli Hull's story of her friend Lilly allow the great grace of Malheur to embrace us with its Milky Way, its timeless waters, and the cycles of life that it so vividly represents. Thus we come to understand and, eventually, accept.

MELI HULL

Desert Sisters

My sister is dead.

Okay, she's not my sister. She's Lucy's sister.

Saying she was Lucy's sister is the quickest way to explain who Lilly was. I could say she was my friend—she was—but that feels inadequate. Calling her my sister now that she's gone makes me feel like I'm trying to claim sympathy I don't deserve. But she was my sister.

She was there for a lot of my growing up, and I was there for a lot of hers. She was my sister because she claimed me as hers. And I think I took her for granted the way you do with a sister. I guess I thought she'd always be there being her weird self.

Lilly drove off the road near where she was living in Dorris, just across the border into the northern tip of California. She rolled her car into an irrigation ditch and drowned. She was twenty-three. A year younger than me.

"On the day she died she texted my dad about how she'd found that geocache at the lava beds," Lucy tells me. "She told him how it reminded her of being in Malheur, and how she loved being out there exploring the desert with her sisters. She used the word 'sisters' right in the text. So you can be comforted by the fact that she really did think of you as a sister, right up to the day she died."

Lucy is my best friend, and I chose her, sort of, as much as you can choose any friend when friends tumble into your life and stick there at random. But I didn't choose Lilly. I was stuck with her, and I wouldn't have had it any other way.

The first time I went to Malheur, I was nineteen. Being sandwiched into Lucy's dad's green 1997 Ford Taurus with her for four days straight was the most time I'd ever spent around Lilly, even though I'd been best friends with Lucy since the first day of high school. Right after this was when Lilly started calling me her sister. Started calling the three of us sisters.

Dave is a pretty well-known birder, and the whole reason we go to Malheur in the first place, and why we call it Malheur, is because of the Malheur National Wildlife Refuge in Harney County. The whole area isn't called Malheur on the map; we call it that because Dave does. He's made the trip every year on Memorial Day weekend to bird since he was a teenager, and when he had kids he brought them too. And then in our first year of college Lucy invited me along.

We left Eugene in the middle of the night so we could get to headquarters just after sunrise, just in time to bird. Lucy and Lilly slept, but I stayed awake the whole way there, listening to the playlist they'd cobbled together the night before. There was a lot of John Prine. I'd never heard of John Prine, then. We stopped at the McDonald's in Burns for lukewarm, flaccid breakfast sandwiches and coffee around six in the morning, and pulled into the Malheur National Wildlife Refuge Headquarters before seven.

Malheur turned out to be a lot of driving fifty-mile stretches through sagebrush between each strange, small desert town, and singing along to country music and oldies, and waiting while Dave pulled the car off on the side of the road every ten feet or so to squint through a telephoto lens as big as your arm looking at birds that were, admittedly, somewhat more colorful than the birds around Eugene. I was fine with it.

We've gone every year on Memorial Day weekend since then, keeping the traditions of Lucy's childhood, even though we aren't birders. Traditions are very important to Lucy. We still stop at headquarters, and we note sandhill cranes, pelicans, red-winged blackbirds, yellow-headed blackbirds, great horned owls, avocets, bobolinks, and burrowing owls when we see them. We also partake in what we call mammaling—which isn't a real thing, for some reason, even though birding is—when we spot ground squirrels, pronghorn deer, coyotes, the cattle that wander the open range, terrifyingly close wild horses, or the pack of burros that lives somewhere near Denio, Nevada. This involves calling out the name of whatever mammal you happen to see and then shouting at the top of your lungs, "*Mammaling!*"

Mostly, we drive around the desert and visit the strange, small towns because we love the place that is Malheur. It's our place.

And it's Lilly's place.

The pictures of her tell that story.

I'm picking pictures to print for the memory table at her memorial. So many of them are from Malheur.

Here she is in the front seat with her feet up on the dashboard in the dusty gravel parking lot at headquarters. Here she is doing a silly pose at the post office in Princeton, because Dave has a tradition of taking pictures outside of post offices in tiny towns. She's tall, with a big grin and long bleached-blonde hair with dishwater roots starting to show. She's posing at Round Barn. She's graceful enough to always be serious, but she never quite is. She's with Lucy down at Fields in the very eastern bottom corner of Oregon, outside the gas-station-convenience-store-liquor-store-post-office-motel-diner with the greatest burgers and milkshakes you'll ever taste, absolutely worth the hundred-mile drive through sagebrush from wherever you are.

She's standing beside the sign for the barely-a-town of Diamond—more accurately an old hotel and surrounding ruins—pointing at the macabre fact of how its population of five is superimposed over a number that was once a seven. She is at headquarters, leaning against the fence looking out over the marsh where pelicans and egrets land. It's the golden hour, and she's bathed in magic pinkish-orangish-gold light. The golden hour's always magic, but it's more magic here. Here she is on the swings at the Frenchglen School, the best swings in the world that let you swing the farthest and the highest ever and make you feel like you're flying absolutely.

I scroll through other pictures of her. The Country Fair, Free Slurpee Day, camping at Indigo Springs. Sleeping in the back seat on the way to the beach. I grin. There she is sleeping on my shoulder while we wait for Lucy's biology graduation to start. That girl could fall asleep anywhere.

At Easter this year.

This year.

It is such a joy, such an act of love to hunt down every picture I can find of her, goofy or beautiful or sassy or all of those. But I'm getting closer and closer to the present—and the present doesn't have her in it. With an awful lurch like being in a car whose driver just slammed her foot down hard on the brakes, I realize there's going to be a last picture of Lilly I ever took. And there are never going to be any more after that.

And I'm about to come up on it.

I open the album called "Malheur 2014" and hold my breath.

Lilly and Lucy around the campfire. Lilly tromping through the old stone ruins in Diamond, tall and proud and fearless. Lilly at the wheel looking serene. I suck in my breath as I realize three months later she dies in that driver's seat.

The three of us standing outside Round Barn, desert sisters. Lilly sitting on the gate looking cute on purpose. With both arms up on the side of the road, showing you the great beauty of the desert all around her. Triumphantly holding up the first geocache she ever found—a Tupperware container with a logbook and tradable trinkets inside—up on the hill above Frenchglen. The view from up there was incredible.

I am getting closer to the end of the album.

She is photo-bombing the picture I'm taking of Lucy holding up a rusty tin labeled in Sharpie on the bottom, "Geocache Catlow Cave." She is smiling next to me as I hold up the list of milkshake flavors at Fields.

She is opening up another geocache: the one at Jean-Baptiste Charbonneau's grave near Danner, Oregon. It's the middle of nowhere even by Malheur's standards, and all of Malheur is the middle of nowhere.

Jean-Baptiste Charbonneau was Sacajawea's son, the only baby born on the Lewis and Clark expedition, a living symbol that the Corps of Discovery came in peace. When he grew up he was a mountain man, a magistrate, a forty-niner, and an interpreter. He was fluent in four languages. On his way from California to Montana toward another gold strike in 1866, he caught pneumonia, and this middle of nowhere is where he happened to be when he died, so this is where they buried him. You end up where you end up.

We drove a full hundred miles from Fields, and fifty of those over awful washboard gravel that had looked on the map like a reasonable road choice. After all that, we almost didn't find the geocache. The rest of us were ready to give up. But she kept looking, and she found it. It was Sunday, the day before we went home.

That's it.

There's a picture of some cows blocking the road on our way back to Frenchglen that evening, which I took because I thought it was great fun to be held up in traffic by cows. And there's a picture of Lucy at the picnic table the next morning, eating straight out of half a watermelon with a plastic spork. Lilly'd brought the watermelon with her, and we didn't end up eating it, and she didn't think she'd be able to eat the whole thing by herself, so she left us with half of it.

When she left. The last time I ever saw her.

I scroll through the few remaining pictures, mostly of me and Lucy holding up geocaches we found on the way home that day. Memorial Day. What if there was some other time Lilly came up to Eugene I'm forgetting about?

There isn't. That's it. The last one is the last one.

There's the tattered American flag I can almost still hear whipping itself around in the wind in the background. There's the big desert sky, and the silent forever expanse of sagebrush all around her.

And there's Lilly. She looks triumphant, calmly. Like she always knew she'd find it. She's proud. She's got that same easy confidence she's always had. She's pure happy.

I'd much rather there not have to be a last picture I ever took of her, but if there does, I'm glad it gets to be this one.

On the morning of the memorial, on the way to Dot Dotson's to print the pictures, by myself in the car, I listen to the Malheur playlist and what I want is to go to Lilly's party, and then, after it's over, to pack the car and drive east.

While Lucy and I are setting up the memory table, Fix, Dave's best friend, comes up to us. He went to Malheur with us the second year I went. Fix is strange: sharply smart and terse, short and wiry and bug-eyed. He knows the Latin names of plants and birds.

"Hello, Lucy," he says. He's a little early. He lives in northern California somewhere and drove up for the memorial.

"Hi, Fix!" She hugs him. "Fix, you remember Meli—"

"You're from Malheur," he says to me, by way of a greeting. I haven't seen him since the trip we took four years ago.

"*You're* from Malheur!"

I am in love with the idea that once you've been to Malheur, experienced it, know everything it means, you are *from* it. You have to have a reason to go there. Everyone who has the great privilege of knowing it is automatically endeared to anyone else who knows it.

"Damn shame about your sister," he says to Lucy.

We make our way out to our tent through the sagebrush-thick night air. We're at Lilly's boyfriend Kenneth's ranch in Dorris. He was throwing a second memorial for the people from Dorris who couldn't make it up to Eugene.

"Lilly pretty much lives in Malheur," Lucy told me the first time she visited Lilly here. It smells like the sagebrush that grows everywhere, and dust, and also, inexplicably, a little like pee. Lucy said I'd see when I got down here that it really did smell like pee. I didn't believe her, but she was right. Is it coyote pee? Dave tells me later it's the smell of western junipers.

The tent is too big for just the two of us. We lay out our sleeping pads at strange diagonals across the tarp floor. The last time we slept in this tent, I realize, was in Malheur, with Lilly. Thinking of that makes me feel closer to her, like she's in here with us. I can almost breathe in the smell of her. Then I think that's ridiculous, because part of why I drove all the way down to Dorris was to be in a place where I would feel like she was. Maybe we could have foregone the drive and set the tent up in the backyard.

I try to sleep.

Now that it's quiet, I suddenly realize how quiet it isn't. There's the constant groan of semitrucks roaring past on the highway near us. Disgruntled cow sounds. The distant yips and yowls and wild children's laughter that is the noise of coyotes doing whatever they do all night. The only other place I've heard this particular crazy sound was in Malheur this past May. I didn't even know what it was then until Lilly told me the next morning. The soft gentle distant call of maybe some owl somewhere, which is a sound I used to hear at night outside my window when I was a kid. And punctuating it all: the continual, irregular electric crunch of bugs flying into the bug zapper on the porch and getting singed to death.

Right side. Left side. Back, staring up at the stars through the mesh of the tent. We left the rain fly off, which is something you can never do in western Oregon. The stars are profuse and bright out here—much more and much brighter than we see in Eugene. My mom and I used to lie outside in the middle of the field in Noti to watch the meteor shower every August. I think this might be even more stars than that.

It makes me happy to think of her seeing these stars. I know she must have loved it. Pitching the tent in the backyard wouldn't have been the same. It wouldn't have had these stars.

After Lilly died, Dave started talking right away about how we were all going to go on a family Malheur trip again next year. Maybe he was the one who planted the idea in our heads that this trip that's a solid seven months away is going to matter so much in the story of what happened after Lilly was gone.

"We've been kind of disproportionately hyped for Malheur, haven't we?" Lucy ponders.

It almost feels like we'll find her there again when we go back. Malheur is the last place, or the last time, I saw Lilly alive. The time is all tied up in the place. And the person is tangled up in the place, too. As much as any person can become a place when they die, Lilly has become synonymous with Malheur. It has become her.

Lilly is synonymous with Malheur. It's appropriate, because the French word *malheur* translates to "misfortune."

We pull into the Steens Mountain Wilderness Resort outside of Frenchglen on the Friday afternoon of Memorial Day weekend after a very long day of driving. Me, Lucy, and her brother Stuart, a year younger than Lilly. The campground's not full, but some birder has gone and camped right in the spot we get every year.

That's the spot where I last saw Lilly. That's where I hugged her good-bye. That's the spot where I always imagine if I'd known I would have held her close a little longer. I know exactly where it was. I stare too long as I walk by the birder's campsite on my way to the water spigot—but I can't go and stand in the spot like I wanted to.

On Saturday morning we drive from Frenchglen to Diamond.

Lucy's mom always says she wants her ashes scattered here when she dies, so I tell Lucy to scatter some of Lilly's here, too.

Lilly said once that if she died, she'd like to have her ashes scattered in a lot of different places. Places she loved, and beautiful places she hadn't been yet. She said she didn't think she'd want to be stuck in one place for-ever. At her memorial, her mom divvied up Lilly's ashes into little plastic containers people could take with them if they wanted, to scatter in places they thought Lilly would like. She's in Oregon and California, of course, but also Pennsylvania, Delaware, New Jersey, New Mexico, Texas, and Hawaii.

Lucy hasn't scattered any of her ashes yet.

We step lightly within the broken stone walls of the ruins. I don't know if it was a church when it was new, but it feels like one now.

"Here you go, Lilly," she says, quiet.

This is the first place we leave her behind.

At Round Barn, here in the middle of the desert quiet, in this little fenced-in patch of bumpy ground in the middle of an endless sea of sage-brush stretching out under a perfect joy-blue sky, it feels like it always does. It feels like this visit is a crepe-paper-thin top layer hovering above all the other brief moments we've visited here on the exact same week-end successive years back into the past. Like time is delicately, floatingly stacked.

Everywhere I look, I can almost see Lilly: grinning, perched on the swinging gate a wind-worn wooden sign warns us to please keep latched. Leaning against the silvery wood of the old barn wall, head thrown back in a reckless laugh. Heckling the groaning cows on the other side of the fence. Reading the informational sign about the cattle baron Pete French and his innovative new barn prototype and his untimely death in a land duel. Racing me and Lucy around the circular inside of the barn—we are caught up in the silliness of pretending to be the horses this barn was built for a hundred and forty years ago. Lilly is the winner.

We only come here for a few minutes every year—it's a great place, but let's be real, there's not that much to see here—and the place never, ever changes, not at all. It's like no time has gone by since the first year I came to Malheur. Here, she still might be alive, might come around the corner of the dark, dusty, light-dotted track with a weird smirk on her face, and you wouldn't be surprised at all. It'd be like she had never been gone.

There's a picture we took here every year: the three of us outside Round Barn. Now, this year, Lucy has her container of Lilly's ashes in the side pocket of her backpack.

"Are we going to take a picture of us at Round Barn holding up Lilly's ashes?" she asks. "Yes. Is it going to be weird? Probably. Are we still going to do it? Absolutely."

"Absolutely," I agree.

I won't share it when we get home, though. It'll be for us, because people who aren't in our strange little family won't understand that this is our sad and funny normal now. They'd get heartbroken looking at it, or they'd think it was weird or in bad taste. They wouldn't get it. It's how it is.

The three of us drive to meet Dave, his partner Shawneen, and Fix at the refuge field station. Dave wants to scatter some of Lilly's ashes up at the top of Coyote Butte.

"I'm not sure if I want to touch Lilly's ashes," I say. I haven't, yet.

"Oh, you should!" says Dave. "You definitely should."

It's a dead body, right? It's dead *Lilly*. If I touch it, some of it'll stay on my hands, and that's gross. And then what? Do I wash it off? Don't some of Lilly's ashes get inadvertently scattered down a bathroom sink in the field station?

"It's kind of cool!" Dave promises. "There are little pieces of bone in it!" It sounds like something Lucy would say.

I'm not sure if I'm going to, but I do.

We scatter with the wind and not against it. "Otherwise you're gonna get a faceful of Lilly," Dave laughs. Southeast. Lucy, then Dave, then me, then Fix, who licks his finger when he's done, then Shawneen, then Stuart.

"Now we'll never come here without her again," says Dave.

"She was an amazing person," Shawneen says. "Truly."

"A life well lived," says Fix. The way he says it, I think he knows how trite he sounds—how much of an understatement it is, or how meaningless that is. Then he says, out of nowhere: "A lot of people die at seventy-eight on their morphine drip not knowing that barn swallows come north." His mouth is a grim line. "Joke's on them."

Nobody says anything for a second.

Then Lucy says, "And that's what we'll put on your tombstone, Fix!"

"Maybe we should scatter a little of Lilly's ashes on the other side of the butte," Stuart says. "That way she'll be able to look out on the trailers where we stayed when we came here as kids."

On the way back down the hill, Fix tells us about the giant anthill mounds we've seen: "The ants collect all these little pebbles from the desert and pile them up like this. After the colony dies, or moves away, these mounds might stay here for a hundred years."

Lucy kneels down to look close. "That's crazy!"

Then, once we're back on flat ground, Fix finds something he's been looking for: the tiniest sagebrush he's ever seen. It's like a little coral, only that scrubbed-raw, delicate, seafoam-green color, and as small as a cat's paw.

"Sagebrushes can live to be two hundred years old," he tells us.

Sagebrush is so ubiquitous out here that I hadn't thought of them as individual sagebrushes, just as an ocean. How old is a sagebrush? It's not the kind of thing you think about. When you make your own path through sagebrushes, though, you find out some of the big ones are taller than you are. When you're driving past, you see it as flat as far as you can see, but when you're in it, it swallows you up.

Lucy grins. "Part of what I love about Round Barn is that the view of the area around the barn with all the sagebrush and the occasional cow on the other side of the fence isn't much different from the view Pete French would have seen forever ago, back in the day. But I didn't think about the fact that I could actually, literally be seeing the same sagebrush that Pete French saw!"

Fix glows at his tiniest sagebrush.

"Here it is! I'm so excited! I want to water it or something, but that would be interfering!"

Dave wanted to get a memorial bench for Lilly and put it on the lawn at headquarters, but he's ridiculous, so he didn't look into ordering the bench until a couple weeks before Malheur. There's no way to get a custom-ordered bench made and shipped that quick. We had to plan a second, shorter trip over Labor Day weekend to set up the bench. Bench Malheur. It's a whole thing.

"Oh my god, I can't believe what it says on the bench," Lucy tells me the day before we leave.

"What does it say?"

"It says, '*Lillian Irons, 1991–2014*,' and then it says '*In loving memory of our desert sister.*'"

I don't know what I expected the bench to say, but I couldn't have imagined anything as good as that.

"I know! Apparently they thought he meant to type 'dearest' instead of 'desert.'" She laughs. "I swear to God, if we get there and the bench says '*Our dessert sister . . .*'"

"Our dessert sister! There's just a picture of a cake engraved into the bench . . ."

"I pretty much had an emotional breakdown last night," Lucy tells me in the passenger seat. The sun is coming up. Filberts crackle underneath my tires as I pull out into the street. We're on our way to pick up Stuart and head east again.

"I was crying, like, 'I don't wanna go on this trip, this is the closest thing we've had to a gravestone for Lilly, I'm not prepared for this kind of closure . . .' It all turned out fine, though."

Then again, we're barely out of the driveway. Nothing has turned out fine yet.

She says all of this like it's no big deal. Like it's totally reasonable for her to have all these feelings, which it is, and also like they're kind of funny, which they are. Funny and true.

When we get to headquarters we find Dave in the back room of the little gift shop, lying on the floor fastening screws underneath a mostly complete memorial bench.

It's a really good bench. Most memorial benches just have a discreet little metal plaque on them or something—but our text is engraved in massive Times New Roman across the entire top slat of the bench. It's magnificent.

We get to headquarters on Sunday morning before Dave, Shawneen, and Kenneth do. It's chilly this morning—it never gets this cold when we come in May. I lie on the stone wall at the bottom of the lawn down by where we're going to put Lilly's bench, soaking up the sun. I pretend I'm a lizard.

And then Dave and Kenneth are carrying the bench down the lawn in the morning sunlight and they're wearing faded jeans and old sweatshirts and baseball caps but I'm thinking about them being pallbearers.

We never got the closure of going to Lilly's grave, because Lilly doesn't have a grave. There's no memorial stone where we can visit her on her birthday or the anniversary of her death. That's a normal experience people have when they lose someone they love. It's in all the movies.

All we've had is ash-scattering, which, if you think about it, is actually the opposite of visiting a grave or a memorial. Instead of creating a specific place you can always come back to where you can think your somber thoughts about death and remember a life well lived, et cetera, you throw all you have left of the person to the wind.

But this bench is physical, almost literal set-in-stone proof that she really is dead, forever.

"Is here good?" Kenneth asks.

They're holding the bench in front of the ribs-high wall. It comes around a little corner, like it's cradling the bench. They scoot it right up into the corner.

"It's almost like we've got a little end table action going on over here," Dave says.

Everybody nods. It's a good place. They set it down.

"I think it's crooked," says Stuart.

"Get out of the way, Rozi," Shawneen laughs. The dog has managed to fit herself between the bench and the wall. "She likes it back there already. Get out of there, Rozi." Rozi doesn't, but nobody minds. Kenneth and Dave shuffle around trying to straighten the bench, but the ground is uneven here. Hesitant, they step away to assess their work.

"Get out of there, Rozi," Shawneen says again, absentminded, as I pull out my camera, but I like the picture better with Rozi peering up through the empty bench. She's wearing a doggie smile—not a great big toothy tongue-hanging-out grin like you're probably thinking. The subtlest, slyest doggie smile you've ever seen.

"Get one of the view from the bench," Lucy tells me.

There's the fence Lilly and I posed on when we were bored, waiting for Dave to finish birding in the golden hour. Tall grass, and the lake where the water birds land. Marsh, and then flat yellow ground for as far as you can see. The big old quiet, blue Malheur sky I love.

We're sitting on the bench, Lucy and me.

Dave looks at the ground. "Now, I'm not going to make any big grand speech or anything, but—"

"You're not going to make a speech, but you're going to make a speech?" Lucy grins up at him. He's always doing that. He did it at Lilly's memorial, too.

"But I just wanted to say, you know, the reason I wanted to get the bench here, it's mostly for you guys."

Lilly called us her desert sisters, and now she's our desert sister forever. It's perfect.

Lilly's Bench. Photo by Meli Hull.

"I have my own memories of Lilly, and I have my own memories here, years of them, and a lot of those are from before Lilly was even born. But I wanted to put the bench here because I know you share a lot of memories with her here."

Stuart wants to find a way out onto the Alvord salt flats. Personally, as the driver, I'm not thrilled about driving on any more gravel roads than I have to. But Stuart so seldom speaks up that when he voices a request, you have to do whatever he wants. That's how it works.

When we step out onto the salt flats, it's like stepping into another dimension. It's absurdly quiet. Malheur has this certain quiet to it whenever you step out of the car anywhere in it—it permeates you—but this is something else.

"I feel like we just stepped into the set for some purgatory in some movie," Lucy says.

Way off across the distance on the other side of the salt flats, there's a blue-purple-black-white-grey ridge. It looks so far away you could probably never get to it. Like the end of the world.

"I wish I could just keep walking," I say, not really to anybody.

It reminds me of how it feels to swim in the ocean. I could do it forever—always keep swimming out a little farther to meet one more wave. Except eventually I'd get hungry and tired and drown, right? But I'd die happy. This feels like that. Like it's *too* good. Even though I'm here now and it's so quiet and holy and fantastic—I know we'll have to climb back up the washed-out dirt track and get back in my dusty car and drive the hundred miles back to Burns. I know I can never get enough of this to be done with it. It's so good it rips a hole in me.

When Lilly was alive, she could never stay in one place for too long. Now I imagine her always speeding through the desert, always on another adventure. She gets to keep swimming farther and farther out into the ocean without ever getting tired; she gets to keep walking long enough to find out what's on the other side of those hills. I know this isn't what being dead is—but I bet if I could just keep going far enough out there into the forever, I bet that's where I'd find her. This place is hers. This is how it is for my sister Lilly.

Epilogue: Closing the Circle

Germany 1944/Malheur 2002: *Tod und Verklärung*

This book contains essays by Dave Marshall and Hendrik Herlyn. They met during the *Birds of Oregon* book project of 1998–2003. Hendrik wrote the white-crowned sparrow account. Dave, who was one of the first biologists to work at Malheur, was the senior editor.

At one point, Dave's background as a nineteen-year-old ball-turret gunner in B-17s over Germany during the closing year of World War II was mentioned. Hendrik, with a twinkle in his eye, said that his father had been among the teenage conscripts brought late into the war to operate antiaircraft batteries for the Wehrmacht.

It is entirely possible that Dave Marshall's B-17 and Habbo Herlyn's battery exchanged ordnance, just as Richard Hugo's bomber rained bombs on the five-year-old Charles Simic as he dashed through the streets of Belgrade, which they later discussed over a San Francisco lunch in 1972 as two of America's most respected poets.

In September 2002, Habbo and Elisabeth Herlyn made their second visit to Malheur National Wildlife Refuge, all the way from Germany, guided by their son.

Adapted from Afield: Forty Years of Birding the American West, *by Alan Contreras*

| Derivations and Permissions

ART

Art by the late Ursula K. Le Guin is copyrighted by the artist's estate and is used with permission. These sketches originally appeared in *Out Here: Poems and Images from Steens Mountain Country*, Roger Dorband and Ursula K. Le Guin, (Raven Studios, 2010). Reprinted by permission of Curtis Brown, Ltd.

ESSAYS

Portions of "The German Visitors" extracted from the journals of Charles Emil Bendire are in the public domain and are reprinted from *Proceedings of the Boston Society of Natural History*, Vols. 18 (1876) and 19 (1877). Hendrik Herlyn's portion appears here for the first time in publication.

Extracts from "The Great Pilgrimage" from *Afield: Forty Years of Birding the American West* (Oregon State University Press, 2009) by Alan L. Contreras are reprinted in the introduction with the author's permission.

"Malheur Then and Now" by Ira N. Gabrielson is reprinted from *The Bird-watcher's America* (McGraw-Hill).

"Prize of the 48 States" by David B. Marshall is reprinted from *Memoirs of a Wildlife Biologist* (2010), privately printed, with permission of the author's family.

"John Scharff's Malheur" is transcribed from a video recording made by Tom McAllister and the late Dave Marshall. It appears here with permission of McAllister.

"My Summer in Paradise" by Tom McAllister is reprinted from *Oregon Birds* vols. 38(2):96 (2012) and 39(2): 72 (2013) with the author's permission.

"The Marshes of Malheur" by Dallas Lore Sharp is in the public domain and is reprinted from *Where Rolls the Oregon* (Houghton Mifflin, 1914).

"Malheur in Winter" by Noah K. Strycker was published in the November 2017 issue of the newsletter *Malheur Musings* published by Friends of Malheur National Wildlife Refuge.

"High Centered" is the preface to Ellen Waterston's book *High Centered: the Oregon Desert Trail as a National Metaphor* (University of Washington Press, forthcoming 2021).

POEMS

"Kiger Gorge" by Alan Contreras first appeared in the chapbook *Fieldwork* (2002) and was reprinted in *Night Crossing* (2004) and *Firewand* (2014). It is excerpted here with the poet's permission.

"Malheur at 14" by Alan Contreras first appeared in the chapbook *Fieldwork* (2002), a fundraiser for the Malheur Field Station, and was reprinted in *Night Crossing* (2004) and *Firewand* (2014).

"Life List" by Quinton Hallett first appeared in *Kwinnim Poems*, vol. 1, 1998.

"Wild Geese" by Ada Hastings Hedges is reprinted from *Desert Poems* (Metropolitan Press, Portland, 1930). It also appears in *Collected Poems of Ada Hastings Hedges*, in preparation 2019, Alan Contreras and Ulrich Hardt, eds.)

Selections from *Steens Mountain Sunrise: Poems of the Northern Great Basin* (Sweetbriar, 2003) by David Hedges are reprinted here with the poet's permission.

"*Artemisia tridentata*" by Ursula K. Le Guin is reprinted from *Late in the Day* (Copper Canyon Press, 2018) with the poet's permission.

"Desert Lessons" by Ursula K. Le Guin is reprinted from *Out Here* (Le Guin and Roger Dorband, Raven Studios, 2010) with the poet's permission.

"Harney County Catenaries" by Ursula K. Le Guin is reprinted from *Late in the Day* (Copper Canyon, 2018) with the poet's permission.

"Malheur before Dawn" from *Even in Quiet Places*, Copyright ©
1996 by The Estate of William Stafford. Reprinted with the permission
of The Permissions Company, Inc., on behalf of Confluence Press, www.
confluencepress.com.

"The Poet in the Desert" by C.E.S. Wood originally appeared in 1915,
was revised and reprinted in 1918, and is in the public domain. The original was reprinted in *Collected Poems of C.E.S. Wood* (Vanguard, 1949). The
selection included here from the 1915 edition is a very small portion of
the original, which is 132 pages long in the 1949 printing.

"Up in a Cottonwood" by Ursula K. Le Guin is reprinted from *High
Desert Journal* (2006) and also appeared in *Incredible Good Fortune* (Sham-
bhala, 2006) and *Out Here* (Raven Studios, 2010). It is used here with the
poet's permission.

Bibliography

Aikens, C. M., and M. D. Couture. 1991. "The Great Basin." In *The First Oregonians*, edited by C. Buan and R. Lewis, 21–26. Portland, Oregon: Oregon Council for the Humanities.

Aikens, C. M., and R. L. Greenspan. 1988. "Ancient Lakeside Culture in the Northern Great Basin: Malheur Lake, Oregon." *Journal of California and Great Basin Anthropology* 10 (1):32-61.

Brimlow, G. F. 1951. *Harney County, Oregon, and Its Range Land*. Portland, Oregon: Binford & Mort.

Burns Paiute Tribe. 1995. *The History of the Wadatika Band of Northern Paiute*. Burns, Oregon: Burns Paiute Tribe.

Canfield, G. W. 1983. *Sarah Winnemucca of the Northern Paiutes*. Norman: University of Oklahoma Press.

Jenkins, D. L., L. G. Davis, T. W. Stafford Jr., P. F. Campos, B. Hockett, G. T. Jones, L. S. Cummings, C. Yost, T. J. Connolly, R. M. Yohe II, S. C. Gibbons, M. Raghavan, M. Rasmussen, J. L. A. Paijmans, M. Hofreiter, B. M. Kemp, J. L. Barta, C. Monroe, M. T. P. Gilbert, and E. Willerslev. 2012. "Clovis Age Western Stemmed Projectile Points and Human Coprolites at the Paisley Caves," *Science* 337 (6091): 223–228.

Jenkins, D. L., L. G. Davis, T. W. Stafford, P. F. Campos, T. J. Connolly, L. S. Cummings, M. Hofreiter, B. Hockett, K. McDonough, I. Luthe, P. W. O'Grady, K. J. Reinhard, M. E. Swisher, F. White, B. Yates, R. M. Yohe II, C. Yost, and E. Willerslev. 2013. "Geochronology, Archaeological Context, and DNA at the Paisley Caves." In *Paleoamerican Odyssey*, eds. K. E. Graf, C. V. Ketron, and M. R. Waters, 485–510. College Station, Texas: Center for the Study of First Americans.

Langston, N. 2003. *Where Land & Water Meet: A Western Landscape Transformed*. Seattle: University of Washington Press.

Louie, M. 1989. "History of the Malheur Paiutes." In *A Lively Little History of Harney County*, 5. Burns, Oregon: Harney County Chamber of Commerce.

Zinn, H., and A. Arnove. 2015. *A People's History of the United States*. Thirty-fifth anniversary edition. ed. New York: HarperPerennial.

| *Contributors*

CHARLES EMIL BENDIRE (1836–1897) was a military doctor assigned to early expeditions by white settlers into the Great Basin. He was born in what is now Germany and moved to the United States in 1853.

CHAS BIEDERMAN graduated from Crane Union High School in 2004 after living with Warren and ZoeAnne Matthews for a year and a half. Between 2009 and 2014, Chas packed and fixed fences for the Bureau of Land Management on Steens Mountain. Chas currently shoes horses in the Portland area.

GREG BRYANT is a writer and computer scientist living in Eugene, Oregon. He is the editor of *Rain* magazine, which reports on community projects and initiatives.

SEAN BURNS is a recent graduate of Siuslaw High School in Florence, Oregon, and is a student at the University of Wisconsin-Stevens Point.

ALAN L. CONTRERAS is co-editor of *Birds of Oregon* (Oregon State University Press, 2003) and has published numerous other works including *Afield: Forty Years of Birding the American West* (Oregon State University Press, 2009) and *Pursuit of Happiness: An Introduction to the Libertarian Ethos of C.E.S. Wood* (Oregon Review, 2014).

HARRY FULLER is a writer, nature guide, and retired broadcaster. His work includes *Great Gray Owl* and *Freeway Birding San Francisco to Seattle*. His birding blog is at atowhee.blog.

IRA N. GABRIELSON (1889–1977) worked as a professional biologist and was the first director of the US Fish and Wildlife Service.

QUINTON HALLETT is a poet based near Noti, Oregon. Her work includes *Mrs. Schrödinger's Breast* (UtteredChaos, 2015), *Refuge from Flux* (Finishing Line, 2010); *Shiver Quench Slake* (Fern Rock Falls, 2004), and *Quarry* (When The Sun Tries, 1992).

ADA HASTINGS HEDGES (1884–1980) was a teacher and well-known Oregon poet. Her collection *Desert Poems* is sometimes viewed as a response to C.E.S. Wood's *Poet in the Desert*.

DAVID HEDGES (no relation of Ada) is a poet based in West Linn, Oregon. His work includes *Steens Mountain Sunrise: Poems of the Northern Great Basin* (Sweetbriar, 2003), *The Wild Bunch* (1998), and *Petty Frogs on the Potomac* (1997).

HENDRIK HERLYN was born in Germany and is a long-time resident of Oregon, where he serves as editor of *Oregon Birds* magazine and as a member of the Oregon Bird Records Committee.

MELI HULL is a writer who grew up in Noti, Oregon, and lives in Eugene. Her work has been published on The Metaworker and in the *Eugene Weekly*. Once a year, she drives to the desert.

WILLIAM KITTREDGE is a retired professor of writing. He is author of a collection of essays, *Owning It All* (1987), about the modern West. He is most well-known for *Hole in the Sky: A Memoir* (1992). His book *The Nature of Generosity* discusses sustainability, civilization, and its relationship to culture, history, and human nature. He was also co-producer of the movie *A River Runs Through It*.

URSULA K. LE GUIN (1929–2018) was one of the world's best-known fiction writers as well as an accomplished poet and artist. She visited the Malheur-Steens region for nearly fifty years and had a special fondness for the Diamond Valley and McCoy Creek area. She died shortly before this collection went to press. She asked that her honorarium for this book be given to the Friends of Malheur National Wildlife Refuge.

MAITREYA works as a Fire Lookout for the USDA Forest Service. He is a singer, photographer, and naturalist who spent many years living in the hamlet of Fields just south of Steens Mountain. He served as an intern at Malheur NWR in 1997.

DAVID B. MARSHALL (1926–2011) was a biologist at Malheur National Wildlife Refuge in the 1950s and went on to a long and successful career in the US Fish and Wildlife Service. He was senior editor of *Birds of Oregon* (Oregon State University Press, 2003).

JOHN F. MARSHALL spent childhood years at the refuge as the son of biologist Dave Marshall. He is a professional photographer based in Wenatchee, Washington.

TOM MCALLISTER was a principal outdoor writer for the *Oregon Journal* and *The Oregonian*. He died as this book was in publication.

THOMAS C. MEINZEN grew up in Eugene, Oregon, and began visiting the Malheur-Steens region when he was a child. A summer intern at the refuge in 2016, he is a recent graduate of Whitman College.

DALLAS LORE SHARP (1870–1929) was an American writer and professor widely known for his popular books about the natural world and travel in the United States.

WILLIAM STAFFORD (1914–1993) was a professor of writing at Lewis and Clark College in Portland, Poet Laureate of Oregon (1975–1993), and also held the role of Consultant in Poetry to the Library of Congress in 1970-1971, a position retitled Poet Laureate in 1985.

NOAH K. STRYCKER is author of *The Thing with Feathers* (Riverhead, 2014), *Among Penguins* (Oregon State University Press, 2011) and *Birding Without Borders* (Houghton Mifflin Harcourt, 2017). When at home he lives in rural Lane County, Oregon.

PETER WALKER is a professor of geography at the University of Oregon. His professional interests are the social and political dimensions of human uses of the physical environment, with a focus on Africa and the American West. His book *Sagebrush Collaboration*, which explores the reaction of Harney County to the Malheur takeover in 2016, was published by Oregon State University Press in 2018.

ELLEN WATERSTON is a writer based in Bend, Oregon. Her work includes *Between Desert Seasons* (Wordcraft of Oregon, 2008), *Via Lactea* (Atelier 6000,2013), *Hotel Domilocos* (Moonglade Press, 2017) and *Where the Crooked River Rises* (OSU Press, 2010). She is the founder of the Waterston Desert Writing Prize and the Writing Ranch.

CHARLES ERSKINE SCOTT WOOD (1852–1944) was a military officer in the American west in the late 1800s. He is best known as the person who transcribed Chief Joseph's surrender speech and later befriended Joseph's family. He was an author of many articles and books, the best known of which are *Heavenly Discourse* (1927) and *The Poet in the Desert* (1918).